The Rise and Fall of Liberal Protestantism in America

The Rise and Fall of Liberal Protestantism in America

David R. Carlin

WIPF & STOCK · Eugene, Oregon

THE RISE AND FALL OF LIBERAL PROTESTANTISM IN AMERICA

Wipf & Stock
An Imprint of Wipf and Stock Publishers
199 W. 8th Ave., Suite 3
Eugene, OR 97401

www.wipfandstock.com

PAPERBACK ISBN: 978-1-6667-3657-1
HARDCOVER ISBN: 978-1-6667-9509-7
EBOOK ISBN: 978-1-6667-9510-3

03/22/22

This book is for my grandchildren:
Brigid, Luke, Daniel, and Mary

Contents

1

Introduction

FROM THE TIME OF the first English settlements in the early 1600s, and for centuries thereafter, the country that was then British America and would eventually become the United States of America had a dominant religious worldview—Christianity; more specifically, Protestant Christianity. But this dominance seems to be ending. The dominant, or at least very nearly dominant, worldview in the United States today is a kind of atheism or near-atheism that may be called "secular humanism." Or, if we wish to name it after the factor that is most influential in it, it may be called "atheistic humanism." It seems to be on its way to replacing not just Protestantism but Christianity in general (including Catholicism, Eastern Orthodoxy, and Mormonism) as the commanding "religion" in the USA.

When I say this atheistic or semi-atheistic worldview is now "dominant or very nearly dominant," I don't mean that it is numerically the most common worldview. No, most Americans still call themselves Christians. And most of those who are *not* Christian—Jews, Muslims, and so on, along with persons who describe themselves as "spiritual but not religious"—would say that they believe in God; they would claim to be theists, not atheists.

Why, then, do I say that secular/atheistic humanism is now the "dominant or very nearly dominant" worldview in the USA? For a number of reasons.

- Not all secular humanists are hardcore atheists; many of them are agnostics. But most agnostics (at least in America today) are virtually indistinguishable from outright atheists except for their reluctance to apply the word "atheist" to themselves. Why are they thus reluctant? For a few reasons: (a) "atheism" has always been something of a dirty word in the USA; (b) they don't want to shock friends and relatives who think atheism is a dangerous mentality; and (c) absent a mathematical proof, how can anybody be absolutely *certain* that God does not exist?

- Secular humanism is the taken-for-granted worldview among many, perhaps most, of those who control America's most influential institutions of propaganda. I have in mind such command posts of American popular culture as the entertainment industry, the mainstream journalistic media, our best colleges and universities (including law schools), and the Democratic Party. It is also by and large the dominant view of those who control our public schools. It is these people, our "masters of propaganda" as they may be called, who have great power to shape American beliefs and values, especially the beliefs and values of young people.

- Great numbers of religiously liberal Protestants (as opposed to religiously conservative Protestants) are, for all practical purposes, secular humanists. Despite claiming to be Christians, and for the most part honestly believing that they are Christians, they "lean" heavily, very heavily, in the direction of secular humanism. This can be seen in the many instances in which, when they come across a fight between conservative Protestants and secular humanists (fights for example about school prayer, abortion, same-sex marriage, transgenderism, sex education in schools), liberal Protestants take the side, not of their evangelical fellow Protestants, but of secular humanists. These liberal Protestants attempt to blend what they regard as the best of traditional Christianity with what they see as the best of secular humanism, thereby producing a "new and improved" version of Christianity. The result in most cases is a blend that is 10 percent old-time religion and 90 percent secular humanism. These liberal Protestants have watered down the strong drink of traditional Protestantism with gallons of secular humanism.

- A high percentage of Americans who call themselves Christians are "soft" in their commitment to Christianity, while a high percentage of those who are secular humanists are "hard" in their commitment to secular humanism. As history has demonstrated ten thousand times, a relatively small group of "hard" believers can outfight a much larger group of "soft" believers—just as, in the days of the Wild West, a handful of determined bandits could rob three or four hundred train passengers. Secular humanism, like Christianity and Islam, is a missionary "religion," and at the moment its missionaries are having tremendous success in spreading their "gospel."

- Secular humanism is especially popular among our younger generations. Why? Because of two of its essential values: personal liberty and "social justice." (a) Personal liberty offers young people sexual freedom (along with the freedom to use recreational drugs), a freedom that is particularly attractive to the young, who are by nature full of sexual energy. (b) Social justice gives them a "cause" to fight for, and this cause entitles them to feelings of moral superiority.—By contrast, secular humanism is *not* very popular among older persons (people, for example, like the old man writing this book). But we old people are, of course, dying off, as is the way with old people. Young people continue living, and in a few years they will be running the country and almost all of its important institutions; and if as they grow older and somewhat more conservative they retain even a small portion of the beliefs of their younger days, they will move American further and further in a secular humanist direction.

- Above all, secular humanism has the "big mo"—momentum. For decades now, American culture has been drifting in the direction of secular humanism, which usually includes a somewhat incoherent blend of personal liberty and socialism. Think, for example, of how readily Americans generally have accepted sexual freedom, abortion, homosexuality, same-sex marriage, and transgenderism; and many among today's young people seem to be accepting the notion that socialism is a fine thing. In recent years, movement in this leftist direction has been accelerating. Many people, especially young people, have the feeling that "everybody" is going there, and that if I myself don't go there, there must be something wrong with me.

In sum, if secular humanism is not yet the worldview of the numerical majority of Americans, it is moving rapidly in that direction.

⟋⟋ ⟍⟍

How did we get here? How did America go from being a thoroughly Christian country to being a country which is today on the verge of embracing atheism or semi-atheism? That's the question this book will try, at least partially, to answer, and it will do so by focusing on the history of two developments.

1. The rise of anti-Christianity in America, and in particular three great anti-Christianity ideological movements: deism (eighteenth century), agnosticism (nineteenth century), and, in the twentieth century, the sexual revolution.

2. Liberal Protestant responses to these three anti-Christianity movements. Again and again liberal Protestantism has adopted a policy of strategic withdrawal (retreat), giving away more and more Christian doctrine in order that it might better retain what it considers to be the essence of Christianity. The end result is that in today's version of liberal Protestantism

very little, if any, Christianity is left. Liberal Protestantism has become the helpmeet of secular humanism.

Let me note four things.

First, when I say that early America was a "thoroughly" Christian country I do not mean to suggest that *all* Americans in that early period were pious, church-going Christians. Far from it. Many were not church-going; many were not pious; many were plain villains. America has always been, and still is today, a country with great multitudes of people who behave rather badly: many of them are downright criminals, many others are not quite criminal themselves, but provide an atmosphere of tolerance in which criminality can flourish: they are the semi-criminal sea in which criminal fish can swim. But in early America even the least pious, if asked to name their religion, would with few exceptions have answered "Christian"—and by "Christian" they meant "Protestant." And if you had asked them if God had given mankind a holy book, they would have answered, "Yes, the Bible"—even if they had never read a single page of the Bible.[1]

Second, when I say that I will try "partially" to answer the question of how we got from Christianity to something very like atheism, I mean that I won't be attempting a *complete* answer. That would require a much bigger book that I am prepared to write. To give a complete answer to the question, I would have to discuss a great number of social, economic, and political factors. In this book I will largely (but not entirely) skip those factors and keep my focus on ideological factors, that is, philosophical or theological factors. I will look at a series of ideological revolutions—deism, agnosticism, and the sexual revolution—that have gradually, over a more than two-hundred-year period, served to undermine American Protestantism.

Third, when I speak of persons who are "liberal" in their Protestantism, I mean people who, while professing—and in most cases

---

1. It is perhaps worth noting that many villainous persons give the same answers today. Our prisons are full of such "Christians." And so the enemies of Christianity usually have no trouble arguing, as they often do, that Christianity and villainy are compatible.

sincerely professing—to be Protestant Christians, feel free to modify that religion in order reduce the apparent contradictions between it and the beliefs and values of the modern secular world. Hence these liberals may also be called "modernists" or "modernizers."

Finally, when I say I'll be focusing on liberal Protestantism, I don't mean to suggest that there have been no liberal forms of Catholicism or Judaism. In the USA Judaism has been more or less liberal since the middle of the nineteenth century, when the first great influx of Jews came to America from Germany, where the Jewish religion had already been "modernized." It wasn't until Jews came into the USA from the Russian Empire (late nineteenth and early twentieth centuries) that Orthodox Judaism became a significant factor in American Jewish life; and most of the children of these Orthodox Jews, as they quickly grew Americanized, soon gravitated either in the direction of liberal versions of their faith or in the still more radical direction of infidelity. As for liberal Catholicism, it was almost nonexistent in American until the late 1960s, following the Second Vatican Council. Since then it has grown and flourished. But Catholics got into the business of being liberal much later than did Protestants, and to this day lag far behind Protestants in their degree of liberalism. Liberal Catholics and Jews aid and abet liberal Protestants. But Protestantism, not Catholicism or Judaism, has been far and away the most important of American religions. And so if I am to tell the story of liberal religion in America, I have no choice but to focus on liberal Protestantism.

2

The Protestant Doctrinal Consensus

PRIOR TO THE PROTESTANT Reformation of the 1500s there was in Western Europe a Christian doctrinal agreement that might be called "the Catholic Consensus."

However, even prior to 1517 (the standard date given for the beginning of the Reformation—for it was in late October of that year that Martin Luther posted his Ninety-five Theses on the church door at Wittenberg) this Catholic Consensus had been showing for more than a century signs of a breakdown, e.g., in John Wycliffe, in Jon Huss, in the Waldensians. But it wasn't until the first half of the sixteenth century that the Catholic doctrinal consensus fell apart, at least in northern Europe, under the theological hammer blows of Luther, John Calvin, and other Reformers, and under the political hammer blows of Henry VIII and other monarchical and republican political authorities.

The Reformation was, among many other things, a rejection of papal authority; and not just papal legislative, executive, and judicial authority, but papal doctrinal authority. According to Catholic teaching, the pope, assisted by the bishops, was the Church's ultimate doctrinal authority. In the 1500s the Roman Church hadn't yet gone so far as to say that the pope was infallible in questions of faith and morals; that declaration didn't come until 1871 at the First Vatican Council. But already in the sixteenth century the Roman church was on the verge of saying this, and for all practical purposes it *was* saying this. In some ways the pope even outranked the Bible in authority. For the Bible, though Catholicism held it to be what Protestantism also held it to be (the infallible word of God),[1] was subject to interpretation; and twenty readers might interpret it, or parts of it, in twenty different ways. Hence an authoritative umpire was needed to judge which of the twenty interpretations, if any, was the correct one. This umpire was the pope.

But if you got rid of the pope, as did the Reformation, who then would be the umpire? Who in a pope-less world would tell us which of the many competing interpretations of this Biblical book or chapter or verse was the correct one? And if we have no umpire, won't doctrinal anarchy ensue? In other words, won't it follow that, the Catholic Doctrinal Consensus being gone, we'll never have a Protestant Doctrinal Consensus?

❧ ❧

To replace the pope as the ultimate doctrinal authority there were in the early part of the sixteenth century a number of possible candidates.

- A church council. This meant a future council, since no council was meeting at the moment; and many reformers, including Luther himself, did in fact appeal to a future council. But this hypothetically possible council never happened. If it had taken place early in the Reformation, it would have been a council made up, in all probability, of a Catholic majority; and it is unlikely that the Reformers would have accepted the rulings of such a council. When, finally, the pope convened a council (the Council of Trent), it was a purely Catholic council, no Protestants in attendance or even invited.

---

1. Though both religious parties agreed as to the infallibility of the Bible, they disagreed as to its contents. Catholics counted as part of the Bible the books that Protestants called "the Apocrypha."

- A council of bishops excluding the pope. (But the pope too was a bishop; so how could he be excluded?) And most bishops were Catholic; so a council of bishops (even one that did not invite the pope) would have been a predominantly Catholic council. Besides, not all forms of Protestantism had bishops; some Protestant churches were organized on a presbyterian or congregational basis. And so a council of bishops never took place.

- A purely Protestant council. This too never happened. But how could it, given the great diversity found among Protestants? Was it conceivable that Protestants generally would submit themselves to the authority of a council made up of Lutherans, Calvinists, Zwinglians, Anglicans, Anabaptists, and Socinians?

- Kings and other secular rulers. Apart from the absurdity of having theology dictated by laypersons lacking deep theological training, this would mean that Christianity would have one form here and another there, depending on the understanding or the wishes or the follies of this or that secular ruler. In England King Henry VIII had some theological learning; it is said that his favorite author was Thomas Aquinas. Besides, the pope had awarded him the title "Defender of the Faith" on account of a tract he had written against Luther in the days before Henry had his falling-out with Rome. But when Henry finally produced his Protestant theological teachings, these satisfied hardly any Protestant or any Catholic in England.

- All the above possibilities having been ruled out, the only remaining possibility was the Bible. The Bible, the whole Bible, and nothing but the Bible would have to be the ultimate religious authority in the post-papal world of Protestantism. Who could object to that? After all, everybody—both the old Christians (Catholics) and the new Christians (Protestants)—agreed that the Bible is the infallible word of God: a God-made book, written by human authors who were operating under the plenary inspiration and guidance of the Holy Ghost. Once you gave up the pope, it made perfect sense that the Bible would be the ultimate doctrinal authority. Besides, it was obvious that the pope, being a mere mortal, could make mistakes; whereas it was equally obvious that the Bible, being a God-make book, could not make mistakes.

Even after all Protestants agreed that the Bible is the ultimate authority, however, there remained this difficulty: in a case when two or more readers of the Bible, especially when these readers were important religious leaders (e.g., Luther, Calvin, etc.), differed in interpretation, who would be the umpire? Who, now that the pope had been dismissed, would decide which is the correct interpretation? The standard Protestant answer to this question was this: If the Bible is read in the correct way, there *will not be* any disagreements between two readers. And what is the correct way? Read it carefully, read it humbly, and above all read it prayerfully, asking guidance from the true author of the Bible, the Holy Ghost. Just as a hundred different arithmeticians, when they do their sums correctly, come to the same answer, so those who read the Bible in the correct way will arrive at the same interpretation. No umpire will be needed.

Here we arrive at the great Protestant principle of private judgment. This was *not* a principle that says we are free to believe whatever we like; likewise, it was *not* a principle that says that there is no such thing as religious truth, and that we are therefore free to hold whatever religious opinions we prefer. Among some latter-day liberal Protestants it may have "evolved" into something like this; but this is certainly not what the early Protestants had in mind. No, they meant that Christian individuals are entitled to read the Bible (the word of God) for themselves, and are entitled, provided they read thoughtfully, humbly, sincerely, and prayerfully, to arrive at their own conclusions.

Catholics objected to this, and not just because they held that the ultimate authority to interpret the Bible resided with the pope and bishops, but also because of what they saw as its likely practical consequences. If every Protestant is free to interpret the Bible, it is inevitable—even if it happens (which it won't) that every single one of them reads the Bible in the "correct" way (that is, carefully, humbly, and prayerfully)—that the result will be a fragmentation of Protestant Christianity. It will be fragmented in doctrine, in morals, in ritual practice, in organizational structure. A single unified Church, headquartered at Rome, will be succeeded by a multitude of churches, sects, and conventicles having no single headquarters and no agreed-upon doctrine.

Now there is no question that the principle of private judgment contributed, and is today still contributing, to the organizational fragmentation of Protestantism. This is especially true in the United States, where almost every day some new variant of Protestantism surfaces, some new sect or conventicle led by a preacher who invokes his (or occasionally her) right to private judgment.

But while this institutional fragmentation is a remarkable thing, even more remarkable is the fact that a Protestant doctrinal consensus that was established five hundred years ago still holds today. More precisely, it still holds in the USA among religiously conservative Protestants, those who call themselves "evangelical" and may be called "old-fashioned Protestants." It no longer holds among those American Protestants who call themselves or are called by others "liberal" or "modernist." The principle of private judgment had the potential for undermining many ancient Christian doctrines, and among liberal Protestants it has in fact undermined these doctrines. But among evangelical Protestants it has, astonishingly, not done this. Whether we should say that this result is *despite* or *because* of this principle, the fact remains that Evangelicals, after half a millennium of religious storm and stress, still adhere to the belief system of early Protestantism.

And what are the articles of belief contained in this five hundred-year-old Protestant Consensus? They are as follows.

- The Bible is the infallible word of God.
- The Bible is the sole authority in religion.

- God is a Trinity of Father, Son, and Holy Ghost.

- Jesus Christ was/is true God and true man.

- Jesus was born of a virgin.

- Jesus suffered and died in atonement for our sins.

- Jesus rose from the dead.

- Human nature was corrupted by the fall of Adam and Eve.

- We humans are incapable of moral goodness without being assisted by the grace of God.

- We receive this grace when we accept Jesus Christ as our Lord and Savior.

- Immediately upon death our souls go either to heaven or to hell.

These articles of belief were spelled out quite explicitly five hundred years ago because in the hurly-burly of the Reformation era there were some people who denied, or might deny, one or another of these doctrines. On the right, Catholics would add to this list of doctrines; on the left, Socinians (Unitarians) would toss out a number of them.

But in addition to these explicit doctrines there were certain *moral* doctrines that didn't need to be explicitly spelled out because they were obviously matters of Christian truth that both Catholics and Protestants could agree on; almost nobody would think of denying them.[2] For example, murder is sinful, and so is theft, and so is lying. Prominent among these moral doctrines were certain teachings related to sexual morality. For example:

- Fornication is sinful.

- Adultery is sinful.

- Homosexual conduct is sinful.

- Polygamy is sinful.

2. That is, nobody in the sixteenth century would think of denying them; in the twenty-first century of course many people deny them.

- Incest is sinful.

- Abortion is sinful.

When we think of a Protestant Consensus, then, we should remember to include these moral doctrines as well.

It helps to bear in mind that Christian doctrine can be divided into three categories: (a) metaphysical doctrines (e.g., God is a Trinity, Jesus Christ is true God and true man); (b) historical-miraculous doctrines (e.g., Jesus was born of virgin, Jesus rose from the dead); and (c) moral doctrines (e.g., that we should love our neighbors, that we should honor our parents, that adultery is sinful, that homosexual conduct is sinful, that theft is sinful). The Protestant Consensus contains all three kinds of doctrine.

We should also remember that there have always been points of disagreement among Protestants who agree in subscribing to the Protestant Consensus. For instance,

- Disagreements as to the validity of infant baptism.

- Disagreements as to the question of predestination.

- Disagreements regarding the nature of the Lord's Supper.

- Disagreements as to the correct form of church government.

Despite these and other disagreements, the Protestant Consensus has held for five centuries—at least it has done so among persons who in the USA are usually called evangelical Protestants.

One of my great aims in this book is to tell, very briefly, the story of how the Protestant Consensus has declined among liberal Protestants for more than two hundred years now until in the early twenty-first century it has almost totally collapsed, leaving liberal Protestantism in a condition in which it is barely distinguishable from outright infidelity.

As I tell this story, I will do so with a thesis in mind. It is my contention that liberal Protestantism in the USA[3] has shown a very

3. And not just in the USA. In this book I will be focused on the USA. But

weak power of resistance to the ideas put forward over the last few centuries by the forces of anti-Christianity. Just the opposite, it has shown a great capacity for accommodating itself to the beliefs and values of these anti-Christianity forces. I shall argue in the pages that follow that there have been three great anti-Christianity assaults in the last 250 years: deism, agnosticism, and the sexual revolution. In all three cases liberal Protestantism has said something like this:

> Hmm, let's think about this. In some ways our critics have a point. Some of our Christian beliefs are wrong, or at least out of date. Shall we therefore abandon our beautiful religion? Not at all. We love Christianity. And the world needs it; especially the United States of America needs it. And so, instead of abandoning it (as our anti-Christianity foes would wish), let us modify it and bring it up to date. Let us keep what is good in Christianity, throwing away what is bad; and let us blend this good with what is good in the beliefs and values of our anti-Christian critics. That will leave us with a new and improved religion, a modernized Christianity.

In fact this process of accommodation to the foes of Christianity has, after more than two centuries of retreat, left liberal Protestantism with almost no religious beliefs at all. Or, to put this in other words, it has left them with a form of "Christianity" that has almost no Christian content. Its doctrinal content today is almost entirely borrowed from the beliefs and values of secular humanism.

---

similar things have happened in Europe and in English-speaking countries other than the USA.

3

Skepticism

AT THE TIME OF the Reformation many European Christians were able to doubt the truth of the Catholic version of Christianity, for if they hadn't been capable of doubting it, they would not have been able to embrace the new religion of Protestantism. And, of course, Catholics were able to doubt the truth of the Protestant version of Christianity. But hardly anybody (apart from Jews, a special case) doubted the truth of Christianity itself. This was something Catholics and Protestants agreed on, that Christianity was the true religion of Jesus Christ—no matter how violently they disagreed as to the correct version of Christianity. But after a generation or two of Catholics shouting that Protestantism is a false religion and Protestants shouting that Catholicism is a false religion, can it be surprising that some people arrived at the conclusion that *both* are false religions? And some people did. A spirit of skepticism arose in Europe. For the first time since the ancient world, skepticism became a live option for a significant number of thinkers; not a great number, but enough to make the world notice.

The best-known of these skeptics was the French philosopher and essayist Michel de Montaigne (1533–92). His great theme was the poverty of human reason and the intellectual modesty that should follow from this poverty; a theme he didn't so much argue for as insinuate in a thousand ways. How little we humans are capable of knowing. How great the gap between what we imagine we know and what we actually know. How small is the gap between human knowledge and the knowledge possessed by our domestic animals. Although Montaigne was a man of the Renaissance in his secular point of view and his devotion to the writers of antiquity, he was quite the opposite of the high Renaissance thinkers and artists in that, whereas they thought human nature was a magnificent thing, Montaigne thought it was rather a poor thing. In this low estimate of human nature, he was not far from the estimate provided by the Augustinian tradition. Unlike the Augustinians, however, whose estimate was based on teachings of the Bible, Montaigne's estimate (and that of Thomas Hobbes, his near-contemporary) was based on empirical observation.

Montaigne's skepticism was so extreme that it led him to doubts, not just about questions of religion and philosophy, but also about that newly emerging thing, modern science. The most burning scientific issue of the day had to do with the question of which astronomical theory was true, geocentrism (the traditional theory) or heliocentrism (the new Copernican theory). Montaigne held that, human reason being so weak a thing, this question can *never* be answered, and that it was only human vanity that made some men imagine it could be answered.

Montaigne was a Catholic, but not because he *knew* or could prove that Catholicism is the true religion of God. He was Catholic because he had been born and brought up in a Catholic family living in a Catholic environment. He freely admitted that if he had been born and brought up in Turkey he would have been a Muslim. He thought it was prejudice, not reason, that gives us our religion.

Montaigne lived during a series of religious civil wars in France (or it could be called, not a *series* of wars, but one long war interrupted by intervals of relative peace). In these wars Catholics (the majority religious group in France) and Protestants (the minority religious group) persecuted and even killed one another

because of religious disagreements.[1] These wars contributed to
the skepticism of Montaigne and others. Since nobody, neither
Catholic nor Protestant nor Jew nor Muslim, actually *knows* what
the true religion of God is, how foolish it is that anybody should
persecute or kill another for not adhering to the "true" religion. It
might make sense to persecute somebody for holding that two plus
two equals five, for when it comes to arithmetic we have genuine
knowledge; but in religion we have only speculation and prejudice.
If we were all skeptics, honestly acknowledging that we don't know
which (if any) is the true religion, we could live in peace with one
another even though we might adhere to different religions. Montaigne may be credited as the "father" of the still-popular theory
that religious tolerance must be based on skepticism.[2]

So significant was skepticism in the French intellectual world in
the generation or two following Montaigne that the two greatest
French philosophers of those generations felt the need to acknowledge this skepticism and fight against it.

1. Rene Descartes (1596–1650) felt that his new philosophy
   would utterly vanquish skepticism by placing philosophy
   and science on a foundation of mathematics-like certainty.
   But the first step he took in pursuing this certainty was to
   carry skepticism to an extreme that even Montaigne hadn't
   imagined. Descartes doubted everything that could possibly
   be doubted, even the existence of the physical universe, even
   the existence of his own body. But he found that it was quite

1. These wars didn't end until King Henry IV issued his Edict of Nantes
(1598), which guaranteed a substantial degree of tolerance to French Calvinists. Henry was a Protestant who, in order to possess his throne with security, converted to Catholicism. "Paris is worth a Mass," he is reported to have
said. One of the greatest of all French kings, his "reward" for having brought
religious peace to France was his assassination (1610) by a Catholic fanatic,
Francois Ravaillac.

2. Roger Williams, the founder of Rhode Island, may be described as the
"father" of the counter-theory that religious tolerance should be based not on
skepticism but on Christian charity.

impossible to doubt the existence of his mind. For doubting is an act of thinking; and one cannot think without having a mind. "I think, therefore I am,"[3] said Descartes. I cannot doubt my own mental existence.

2. Blaise Pascal (1623–62), who was half a skeptic himself, was not persuaded by Descartes, but he argued that the pessimistic conclusions of skepticism could be overcome by a turn to religious faith. Further, in his famous "Wager Argument," he pointed out that it is more reasonable to believe in God, and act on that belief, than to doubt. (a) For if we believe in God and act on our belief (that is, conduct ourselves as good Christians), we are likely (if God really exists) to go to heaven following death, while if we do the opposite we are almost certain to go to hell. The believer who made the correct wager makes and infinite win, while the non-believer, who made the wrong bet, suffers an infinite loss. (b) But if it turns out that God does not exist and there is no afterlife, the believer, who made the wrong wager, suffers, if anything at all, no more than a small loss (he abstains from a few sins he might otherwise have committed), while the non-believer, who made the correct bet, makes, if anything, no more than a small gain (he gets away with committing a few sins).

However, neither the philosophy of Descartes nor Pascal's appeal to religious faith and smart betting were sufficient to crush skepticism. In the eighteenth century it could be found in a number of countries, especially France, where it helped to undermine the old regime of church and state, thus paving the way for the arrival of the French Revolution.

⸎

Now a culture of skepticism, if allowed to grow and expand, will eventually lead to a culture of atheism. There is a logical procession here. If our mind is full of doubts, how can we believe in God? And if we cannot believe in God, doesn't it make sense positively to

3. "Cogito ergo sum," or "Je pense donc je suis."

deny the existence of God? And so an arguable case can be made that the atheism and near-atheism so widespread today in Europe and North America had its beginning, its seed-time, in the French skepticism of the sixteenth century. However, while there may have been *some* outright atheists in the sixteenth, seventeenth, and eighteenth centuries, they were few in number. But if skepticism leads quite naturally to atheism, and if skepticism was present in sixteenth-, seventeenth-, and eighteenth-century Europe, especially France, why were there so few outright atheists?

We might ask a similar question regarding the famous expression found in the Declaration of Independence, "All men are created equal." Why, since this clearly implied that slavery is wrong, did belief in this expression not immediately lead to the abolition of slavery? Why did it take almost another century plus a great civil war to bring this abolition about? The answer: because we humans, though logical or rational beings, are not *purely* logical or *purely* rational, the way a well-made computer is. We are also emotional and egoistic; we tend to cling to our interests and habits, no matter how irrational they may be. Most of us change our beliefs and values only gradually, if we change them at all. It takes time for our concrete convictions to align with our abstract principles.

And so European Christians, both Catholic and Protestant, were generally unwilling to abandon Christianity regardless of skeptical attacks. If the enemies of Christianity wished to undermine and destroy the old religion, they would have to do it gradually, step by step. They would have to begin with something less radical than skepticism and far less radical than outright atheism.

And so the truly effective enemies of Christianity began with deism.

In the next chapter we'll look at deism, the first outright and relatively popular form of anti-Christianity; and the first of the three great anti-Christianity attacks—deism, agnosticism, and the sexual revolution—that I'll be examining in this book.

4

The First Assault

Deism

THE FIRST DEISTIC PHILOSOPHER was an Englishman, Lord Herbert of Cherbury (1583–1648), but it wasn't until the latter part of the seventeeth century that deism gained any real popularity in England. This was almost surely a reaction to the Puritan fanaticism that in the two decades beginning about 1640 had produced a civil war, the execution of a king (Charles I), the abolition of the monarchy, and the military dictatorship of Cromwell. If you hated all that, and millions of Englishmen did hate it, you probably blamed the Puritans. And since the Puritans thought of themselves as the truest of true Christians, you, if you agreed with the Puritan's self-estimate, may well have blamed not just Puritanism but Christianity itself. If so, deism gave you what you wanted. It provided you with a way of believing in God without being a Christian. Subjectively speaking, you may not have *intended* deism as a stepping-stone toward getting rid of Christianity, but objectively speaking that's what it turned out to be.

Deism, after briefly thriving in the late seventeenth and early eighteenth centuries, soon fizzled out in England. The reason for this may be that many Anglicans, especially Anglican theologians, became what we may call semi-deists. That is to say, without abandoning Christianity, they argued that Christianity is a "rational" or "reasonable" religion. This was their "refutation" of deism. For deists said that religion must be rational, and they asserted that deism was the one and only rational religion. But the rationalistic Anglicans argued that Christianity itself was rational and that, therefore, there was no need to reject Christianity and turn to deism. A great example of this is a book by the famous and tremendously influential philosopher John Locke (1632–1703), *The Reasonableness of Christianity*. Locke argued that the existence of God can be philosophically proven—by reason. Likewise, the truth of Christianity can be proven—by a careful and rational study of those important historical documents, the four Gospels. If Christianity is a reasonable religion, then Puritanism, with its "enthusiasm" (as Locke called it[1]), is a false form of Christianity; and so there is no need to turn to deism to get away from Puritanism. We can simply be reasonable or rational or moderate (non-enthusiastic) members of the Church of England.

If deism tended to fade away in England, it jumped the Channel and flourished in France, where it became the "religion"[2] of anti-Catholic intellectuals (e.g., Voltaire, Rousseau), and where it prepared the ground for, and shaped the anti-Christian character of, the French Revolution. Deism was also found in a number of other places—e.g., Germany, Scotland, northern Italy, even pre-Revolutionary America—but France was its heartland.

Since deism had no Bible and no pope and held no ecumenical councils, it had no *official* creed. But it had an unofficial creed, for

1. See chapter 19 of Book IV of Locke's magnum opus, *An Essay on Human Understanding*, for his denunciation of enthusiastic religion. We today would call it fanaticism, not enthusiasm.

2. Though many deists spoke of deism as a religion, indeed as the only true religion, strictly speaking it was not a religion; for it lacked a number of elements found in actual religions. For instance, it did not have a priesthood, it did not have weekly religious services, etc. It had only two parts of a religion, namely a belief system and a code of morality. And in a way it had a holy book, Diderot and d'Alembert's *Encyclopedia*.

deists were generally in agreement as to the following beliefs. The "Deistic Consensus," it might be called.

1. A Supreme Being (God) exists.

2. God is all-good, all-powerful, all-wise.

3. God created the world and governs it by fixed and unalterable laws of nature.

4. Divine revelation is quite unnecessary; reason alone is sufficient to discover the existence of God and our moral duties.

5. The Bible is a man-made book, not a God-made book.

6. Since the laws of nature are unalterable, God does not produce miracles.

7. Since God produces no miracles, it makes no sense to pray to God for miracles; though it does make sense to offer God prayers of honor and gratitude.

8. There is an afterlife in which we will be rewarded for our good deeds or punished for our bad deeds.

9. God wants humans to be happy in this life.

10. Our fundamental ethical duty is to promote the happiness of mankind.

With regard to Jesus Christ, deists believed the following.

1. Jesus was a good man who taught an excellent system of morality.

2. He was not God.

3. He was not born of a virgin.

4. He did not rise from the dead.

5. He did not suffer and die in atonement for our sins.

6. He did not ascend bodily into heaven.

7. He did not found any of the presently-existing Christian churches.

It is easy to see how deism was arrived at. Its adherents started from Christianity, and then they deleted from it everything that is mysterious or miraculous or supernatural or "superstitious," and what they were left with was deism. But that's not how the deists themselves understood things. They thought that deism was the original and "natural" religion of humankind. Over the centuries, however, wily priests, aided and abetted by power-hungry kings, had added irrational elements to this natural religion in order to get power over religious believers. But now that we deists have stripped away these adventitious elements, we can return to the almost self-evident beliefs of mankind's natural religion.

The great German writer and scholar Gotthold Lessing (1729–81), who was a Protestant touched by deism, once wrote a drama titled *Nathan the Wise*. It was set in Jerusalem during the Crusades. The three main characters were a Christian, a Muslim, and a Jew (this Jew being Nathan, a rabbi modeled on Lessing's friend, the German-Jewish philosopher Moses Mendelssohn—who, by the way, was grandfather to the famous musical composer). The play stressed the elements that all three religions had in common. A deist would say that those common elements constitute natural religion, and that all three religions are invalid insofar as they go beyond natural religion. By contrast, Lessing seems to be saying that all three religions are valid inasmuch as they contain the religion of nature; they are three versions of the one true religion.

It is worth distinguishing between two kinds of deists.

One kind hated Christianity, which they considered to be a very bad thing—religiously, morally, and intellectually. The world, in their opinion, would be better off without it; and the sooner it disappears and is replaced by deism the better. Examples of these virulent anti-Christianity writers were Voltaire[3] and Tom Paine.[4]

---

3. See Voltaire's *Philosophical Dictionary*.
4. See Paine's *The Age of Reason*.

Another kind of deist, while considering Christianity to be inferior to deism, was more benign. Deists of this kind considered Christianity semi-good. For ordinary people who were not capable of rising to the level of deism, Christianity was okay, for it was better than nothing; more particularly, it was better than atheism. Examples of this kind of deist were the great German philosopher Immanuel Kant[5] and Thomas Jefferson.[6]

∽∾

Deism never developed a widespread following in America, yet there were some notable American deists. For example:

1. Thomas Jefferson. While serving in the White House, Jefferson produced a deistic version of the four Gospels, doing this by cutting and pasting. He simply deleted everything in the gospels that a good deist would object to, especially the miracles. What was left after these redactions, Jefferson assumed, was the truth about Jesus and his teachings. This work was published after his death.[7]

2. Benjamin Franklin. See his letter to Ezra Stiles, president of Yale College, written just a few months before Franklin's death. But Franklin's deism, at least in his later years, seems to have been less than complete. For one thing, he thought that prayers asking God's help were at least sometimes answered; if America had, rather miraculously, won its War of Independence, this was in some measure due, Franklin believed, to answered prayers. For another, Franklin had something of an open mind on the question of the divinity of Christ.[8]

---

5. See Kant's *Religion within the Limits of Reason Alone.*

6. See Jefferson's *The Life and Morals of Jesus of Nazareth.*

7. A modern edition of this work was published by Beacon Press in 1989 under the title of *The Jefferson Bible.*

8. For his views on the divinity of Christ, see a crucial passage in his letter to Stiles, to be found at Wikipedia, "Benjamin Franklin," in a section titled "Political, social, and religious views."

3. Tom Paine. It is questionable that Paine should be called an American. He was an Englishman who came to America not long before the beginning of the Revolutionary War, in which he played a very valuable part as a pro-American propagandist. A few years after the war he went back to England, where he tried to promote an English revolution, and after that he went to France to help out with that country's famous revolution. In France he wrote *The Age of Reason*, a furiously anti-Christianity book.

4. Ethan Allen. He was another hero of the Revolution, leader of the Green Mountain Boys who captured Fort Ticonderoga and carried its cannons to General Washington in Boston. After the war he wrote a thoroughly deistic book titled *Reason the Only Oracle of Man; or a Compendious System of Natural Religion.*[9] This was probably the first explicitly anti-Christianity book produced in America.

I said above that deism, despite having some distinguished followers in this country, never really thrived in the United States. One of the great reasons for this is that, beginning in the 1790s and lasting for the next few decades, much of the USA underwent what has been called the Second Great Awakening, a tremendous display of religious revivalism. This pretty much killed off deism.

But it didn't kill it off entirely. For it survived (kind of) as an element of Unitarianism. At the end of the eighteenth and beginning of the nineteenth centuries many Congregational ministers of eastern Massachusetts found deism intellectually attractive—but not so attractive as to make them willing to abandon the religion they loved, Christianity. And so they blended deism with Christianity, the result being a new religion (new, that is, in America, for it had already taken root in England), Unitarianism.

We'll look at that in the next chapter.

---

9. This book was originally published in 1784. In 2005, Kessinger Publishing issued a copy of the 1784 printing.

5

Unitarianism

The Liberal Response to Deism

PRIOR TO THE AMERICAN Revolution, British America, the country that was destined to become the United States of America, was marked by a high degree of religious unity. Despite some Catholics in Maryland and a few Jews sprinkled here and there, almost everybody was Protestant. But there were three kinds of division among Protestants.

1. There were denominational divisions: Congregationalists in most of New England; Baptists and Quakers in Rhode Island; Anglicans and Dutch Reformed in New York; Presbyterians and some Lutherans in New Jersey; in Pennsylvania, Quakers plus some German sectarians (the so-called "Pennsylvania Dutch"); in the coastal areas of all the states south of Pennsylvania, Anglicans; and everywhere in the backcountry far from the Atlantic, Baptists and Methodists.

2. There were divisions regarding church government or polity. A congregational form prevailed in New England, and among Baptists, Quakers, and the Pennsylvania Dutch. A

presbyterian form prevailed among Presbyterians. And an episcopal form prevailed among Anglicans.[1]

3. There was one very significant theological division: Calvinism, which had been colonial America's dominant theology from the earliest years, was gradually giving way almost everywhere to Arminianism, a relatively "soft" modification of Calvinism.

Despite these divisions there was a high degree of doctrinal unity. Virtually all Protestants believed the following—what I called in an earlier chapter the Protestant Consensus.

- The Bible is the infallible word of God.
- The Bible is the sole authority in religion.
- God is a Trinity of Father, Son, and Holy Ghost.
- Jesus Christ was/is true God and true man.
- Jesus was born of a virgin.
- Jesus suffered and died in atonement for our sins
- Jesus rose from the dead.
- Human nature was corrupted by the fall of Adam and Eve.
- We humans are incapable of moral goodness without receiving the grace of God.
- We receive this grace when we accept Jesus Christ as our Lord and Savior.
- After death our souls go immediately either to a place of everlasting blessedness (heaven) or a place of everlasting misery (hell).
- Love of God and love of neighbor are the greatest virtues.

---

1. Soon after the Revolution, the Church of England in the USA figured out, "England" having become a very unpatriotic word, that they had better change the name of their church to "The Protestant Episcopal Church of the United States." Today the official name of this church is "The Episcopal Church."

- Among actions prohibited are: murder, theft, lying, fornication, adultery, homosexuality, abortion.

That was the religious situation prior to the American Revolution. But things soon changed. By the first decade of the nineteenth century, especially in New England, there were two notable groups of dissenters, Unitarians and Universalists. The former denied the Trinity and the divinity of Christ, the latter denied everlasting punishment (hell), and both denied the Calvinist notion of predestination. Compared to the entirety of American Protestantism, these were two relatively small groups, but they represented the beginning of the breakdown of the Protestant Consensus. The Unitarians were the more influential of the two dissenting groups, for Unitarianism was the religion of the socio-economic elite in the city that was at that time America's cultural capital, Boston, and they controlled what was then, and still is today, America's most import institution of higher education, Harvard College (today Harvard University). By contrast, Universalism was a rural and not-very-highly-educated phenomenon. For these reasons, then, I will focus on Unitarianism, not Universalism, in this chapter.

In a way I hate to accuse the early Unitarians of having made a significant contribution to the undermining of Christianity in the USA, for it certainly wasn't their intention to do so. The first generation of Unitarians honestly thought they were contributing to the preservation and improvement of Christianity. They believed they were continuing the work of the Reformers. If the sixteenth-century Reformers thought that they were getting back to the essentials of Christianity, freeing it from certain unwarranted additions that Rome had tacked on to it, the Unitarians thought they were getting rid of even further unwarranted additions. The Reformers, as Unitarians saw things, had got only halfway back to original Christianity. The Unitarians, in their own view, were going all the way back, all the way back to the Christianity of Jesus himself.

Looking back on it, this Unitarian self-conception may seem to us hilarious. The Unitarians imagined, in all sincerity, that the religion introduced by Jesus was a religion that suited the hearts and minds of early-nineteenth-century upper-class Bostonians, the merchants and professional men of the city along with their wives and children, plus of course the Harvard faculty. Only eighteen centuries after Christ did somebody—the "Brahmins" of Boston and their pastors—finally understand what Jesus had been up to. However, no matter how much this may amuse us in retrospect, and no matter what credit we may wish to give the early Unitarians for good intentions, the fact is that by being (along with the Universalists) the first liberal Protestants in America, they initiated the disintegration of the Protestant consensus in the United States. Not only that, but they created the pattern that would be followed by others who later continued this disintegration.

That pattern was this:

1. The liberal Protestant, who is nothing if not open-minded, listens to the criticisms of Christianity made by whatever happens to be the fashionable form of anti-Christianity in his/her day, and concludes that there is some merit in these criticisms.

2. Nonetheless, the liberal Protestant retains a strong emotional attachment to the Christianity of his/her childhood and youth. And so, while conceding that the critics of Christianity make some good points, the liberal Protestant holds that the currently fashionable form of anti-Christianity goes much too far when it totally repudiates the old religion.

3. And so the liberal Protestant attempts to blend two things: the best of Christianity, and the best of the current criticisms of Christianity. The result, the liberal Protestant believes, is an up-to-date form of Christianity; a new and improved form of Christianity.

4. This diminution of the doctrinal content of Christianity is usually accompanied by an intensified emphasis on morality, as though this stress on Christian morality will compensate, or more than compensate, for a decline in traditional

Christian doctrine. The morality in question, however, will not necessarily be traditional Christian morality; indeed, as we will see in the late twentieth and early twenty-first centuries, it may even be the opposite.

This pattern is well illustrated in the emergence of Unitarianism in late eighteenth- and early nineteenth-century Boston and vicinity.

1. The fashionable form of anti-Christianity in that day was deism. Some of its central criticisms of Christianity had merit (so thought liberal ministers and their followers): for example, its rejection of the Trinity, its rejection of the divinity of Christ, and its rejection of the sinfulness of human nature.

2. Liberal ministers in and around Boston circa 1800, even though they were very unhappy with the Calvinistic Christianity of their boyhood, continued to have strong emotional attachments to Christianity—that is, Christianity rightly understood. It was unthinkable to them that their sympathy with the deistic critique of Christianity would lead them to abandon the dearly loved religion. In their opinion, deism, whatever otherwise its merits, went much too far when it rejected Christianity altogether.

3. Therefore, the Unitarian ministers said, "Let us combine the best of Christianity with the best of the deistic critique of Christianity." The result: Unitarianism.

4. And if the ministers and their people could no longer adhere to many old Christian beliefs, they all the more held on to what they believed to be the essence of Christianity, its love-your-neighbor ethic. They especially demonstrated this in their disapproval of slavery. Pay a visit to Memorial Hall at Harvard to get some idea of how many Harvard men sacrificed their lives in the Civil War. This was in the days when Harvard was still a thoroughly Unitarian institution.

The birthplace of American Unitarianism was Massachusetts. More particularly, it was Boston and its vicinity.[2] In the decades just prior to the American Revolution, many Congregational ministers and their parishioners in eastern Massachusetts—from Portland[3] in the north to Cape Cod in the south—gradually drifted away from Calvinism, the traditional theology of the Congregational churches, and in the direction of an Arminian theology—Arminianism being a not-quite-Calvinist theology, a "softer" theology that allowed for some free will as opposed to strict predestination. And in the decades after the War of Independence many of the parishes of eastern Massachusetts drifted even further away from Calvinism and became Unitarian. This led to many splits in local churches in eastern Massachusetts. The disagreements between Calvinists and Arminians were, so to speak, intramural squabbles. Though disagreeing, they could maintain parochial fellowship with one another. But the disagreements between, on the one hand, Calvinists/Arminians and, on the other, Unitarians was quite something else; a great gulf was fixed between the two. Soon parishioners came to realize that it didn't make much sense for Christians who differed so widely, as did these two groups, to remain members of the same local church. The majority (usually the Unitarians) retained possession of the church buildings; the minority departed and, if they were numerous enough, built a new church building for themselves, often no more than a few hundred yards away from the old church building.

William Ellery Channing (1780–1842), a Boston minister who grew up in Newport and studied at Harvard College, has often been called "the father of American Unitarianism"—not because he was the first American Unitarian (he wasn't), but because he wrote what was in effect the Unitarian Declaration of Independence. This was an 1819 sermon that Channing delivered in Baltimore at the ministerial ordination of Rev. Jared Sparks (who many

2. This gave rise to the witticism that Unitarians believe in "the Fatherhood of God, the brotherhood of man, and the neighborhood of Boston."

3. Up until 1820, when, as part of the Missouri Compromise, it became a separate state, Maine was the large northeastern section of Massachusetts.

years later became president of Harvard College). In this sermon Channing described the beliefs held by a what he called a new class of Christian believers, the people who were calling themselves, and were being called by others, "Unitarians." A few years after this famous sermon was delivered, the Unitarians officially separated from the traditional Congregationalists and formed their own denomination, the Unitarian Association. Until his death Channing remained the best-known, and probably the most influential, of all Unitarian ministers.

In this famous sermon (the official title of which is "Unitarian Christianity") Channing expounded points of contrast between Unitarian beliefs and traditional Christian beliefs.[4]

1. The Bible is a record of "God's successive revelations to mankind, and particularly of the last and most perfect revelation of his will by Jesus Christ." The most important part of the Bible is the New Testament. Anything clearly expressed in the Bible must be believed as the word of God. But the Bible must be read with the same critical tools we use when reading any other book.

2. Rejection of trinitarianism. God is a unity, not a Trinity. The traditional doctrine of the Trinity says in effect that there are three supreme beings, not one. This, says Channing, is tritheism, not monotheism.

3. Rejection of the incarnation. Jesus Christ, though a uniquely good and wise man, was not God. However, Unitarians had two different opinions about this: (a) an Arian opinion, according to which Jesus, though not equal to God the Father, had pre-existed his human incarnation; and (b) a Socinian opinion, according to which Jesus was simply an excellent man who was sent to us by God, but did not pre-exist his human life.

4. "We believe in the *moral perfection of God.*" This entails a rejection of the Calvinist idea that we come into the world as

4. Channing, "Unitarian Christianity."

sinners, either (a) guilty of the sin of Adam and Eve or (b) so prone to sin that we become depraved sinners from the first moment that we have the capacity for sin. For if God is truly good (and he is), God would not create us so.

5. We humans are not born wicked, nor are we born virtuous. We make ourselves wicked or virtuous by our free choices.

6. "We believe that he [Jesus] was sent by the Father to . . . rescue men from sin and its consequences, and to bring them to a state of everlasting purity and happiness." Further, the death of Jesus was an essential part of that mission. But precisely *how* the death of Jesus rescued us is not something all Unitarians agreed on. But what Unitarians *do* agree on is that Jesus *did not* rescue us by "appeasing the wrath of God" or by "paying the price" for human sins (beliefs regarding the atonement held by Calvinists and Arminians). In other words, they rejected the old Anselmian idea of substitutionary atonement.

7. Rejection of the Calvinist doctrine of "irresistible" grace. It may well be that God assists us in our moral strivings, but they must be our own free will strivings; God does not *compel* us to be good.

8. The importance of love. We must have three loves: love of God the Father, love of Jesus Christ our Savior, and love of our fellow humans. We must be careful not to allow one of these loves to distract us from another. And so we mustn't allow our love of Jesus to distract us from love of God. And we mustn't allow love of God to distract us from love of our fellow man.

Some of these Unitarian rejections are rejections of specifically Calvinist doctrines rather than Christian doctrines held by all Protestants, but at least two of them—the rejections of the Trinity and the Incarnation—are quite clearly rejections of doctrine held by Protestants generally, and by Catholic and Orthodox believers too. In other words, these two rejections involve the rejection of traditional Christianity in the broadest sense of that term.

Note well, however, that Channing and his fellow Unitarians did not reject any of the traditional Protestant moral teachings. Among other things, they held on to traditional Protestant ideas about chastity; they deplored fornication, adultery, and homosexuality.

ೲ ൦എ

The leaders of Boston Unitarianism—Channing, Andrews Norton, and others—apparently believed that you can reject *some* classical Christian doctrines and stop there; you could chop off a few big limbs from the ancient Christian tree without running a serious risk that others, inspired by your example, will chop off further branches, and perhaps eventually chop down the entire tree. And so the older Unitarians were shocked when in 1838 Ralph Waldo Emerson delivered his "Divinity School Address" to the graduating class of Harvard's (Unitarian) Divinity School. Emerson had been a Unitarian minister who resigned his Boston pastorate a few years earlier because of some intellectual difficulties with the Unitarian idea of the Eucharist; and now, it turned out, he had difficulties with Christian beliefs generally, including the thin and streamlined version of Christian beliefs held by Unitarians. His address, in addition to having a strong odor of pantheism about it, suggested that there is nothing uniquely special about the Christian religion. It is a true religion, so to speak, but just one true religion among many, and its truth has been misunderstood and misrepresented by its adherents, including its Unitarian adherents. And Jesus ("whose name is not so much written as ploughed into the history of this world") is a godlike man; but so have there been many other godlike men; and so may we ourselves be godlike men.

Well, the Unitarian elders were shocked. Andrews Norton (who was sometimes called "the pope of Unitarianism") was provoked to write an essay on "the latest form of infidelity"—that is to say, Emersonian infidelity. But once you trim the tree of orthodoxy, even though you command (as Norton and other early Unitarians would have commanded), "No further trimming," by your very example you have announced to your friends and followers, "This is a tree that may be trimmed further." And so others will continue to trim, no matter your protests. Eventually it won't be the branches only; it will be the trunk. Given enough time, you will trim so much that there will be nothing left. There is, I contend, a slippery slope that leads logically, once the "trimming" has begun, from moderate departures from Christian orthodoxy, via liberal Protestantism, to atheism. Liberal Protestantism is a kind of motel that one stops briefly at when traveling the highway from Christianity to atheism.

This is the history—and the destiny—of liberal Protestantism, the form of Christianity that feels free to amend, even to delete, doctrines of traditional Christianity in order to make the religion "new and improved," in order to keep it "up to date," in order to be on "the right side of history." Liberal Protestantism is not in itself atheism; often it is very pious and morally very decent. But it *tends* toward atheism—just as an acorn tends toward an oak tree and just as a caterpillar tends toward a butterfly. Atheism, I contend, is the logical conclusion of liberal Christianity. But it is a conclusion only very gradually arrived at. Unitarianism, the first form of American liberal Protestantism, commenced its career somewhat more than two hundred years ago. Only recently, in the early decades of the twenty-first century, has liberal Protestantism arrived at a point where it has become barely distinguishable from outright atheism.

Before looking at further stages of the reaction of liberal Protestantism to fashionable forms of anti-Christianity, let us look at the first reaction to the reaction—that is, the reaction of traditional Protestantism to liberal Protestantism.

6

The Second Great Awakening

I HAVE CONTENDED THAT liberal Protestantism develops as a series of reactions to fashionable forms of anti-Christianity (e.g., deism, agnosticism, sexual revolution), a reaction that consists of a "compromise" between Christianity and anti-Christianity, a blend of the two; and this compromise produces what liberal Protestants have regarded as a new and better kind of Christianity. But there is a second reaction we have to notice—a reaction to the reaction. Traditional Protestants have again and again had a negative reaction *both* to the present-day fashionable form of anti-Christianity (whether that be deism or agnosticism or the sexual revolution) *and* to the liberal Protestant compromise with anti-Christianity.

In the early 1800s traditional Protestants had a negative reaction to deism and, perhaps even more, to Unitarianism. These old-fashioned Protestants re-affirmed their belief in the Trinity, in the divinity of Christ, and in the sinfulness of post-Eden human nature. They also re-affirmed their confidence in the inspirational power of the Holy Ghost, a power that could—and often did—morally transform a person from sinner to saint in an instant. This reaction was what came to be called the Second Great Awakening.

The Second Great Awakening

The original Great Awakening had taken place in the thirteen colonies of British America during the 1740s. It was marked by strongly emotional experiences in response to sermons preached by eloquent and fiery ministers. There were many such ministers, the two best-known being Jonathan Edwards of the Connecticut River Valley and George Whitefield, the English Methodist. These emotional reactions were considered to be "conversion experiences," as sinners, moved by the Holy Ghost, passed through a three-step process: (a) a very lively awareness of their own sinfulness and of their danger of being, on account of these sins, condemned to everlasting damnation; (b) a more or less extended period of extreme anguish, which for some lasted no more than a few minutes while for others it lasted many weeks or months; and (c) a realization (given to them by the Holy Ghost) that they were among the Elect, that is, among those who would spend eternity in heaven, not hell—and from this point forward they could live their lives with easy minds about the greatest of all questions. Unfortunately there were some poor souls who achieved (a) and (b) but never arrived at (c). Their subsequent lives must have been lives of mental misery.

The Second Great Awakening, which took place in the early decades of the nineteenth century, was very like the first Awakening in its emotionalism and in its conviction that these strong emotions were the result of a tremendous outpouring of grace from the Holy Spirit.

But there were some secondary differences. At the time of the first Awakening, it is probable that most Americans who were directly affected were Calvinist in their theology; by the time of the second Awakening, however, more than a half-century after the first, it is likely that most of those directly affected were Arminians in their theology. Calvinism made no allowance for free will, while Arminianism did make such allowance. And by the nineteenth century, Americans, who had won a war of independence, who had settled and civilized the Atlantic seaboard prior to the Revolution and who had begun to settle and civilize the interior of the continent following the Revolution, who had written and adopted a national Constitution following the Revolution—these Americans, conscious of their great accomplishments and aware of their potential for even greater accomplishments, would quite naturally find it awfully hard to believe that they lacked free will. Maybe Russians and Chinese lacked free will; but certainly not Americans. The somewhat newer Arminian theology must have seemed far more plausible to them than the older Calvinist theology.

Again, the earlier Awakening had taken place when America was a far less populous place than it had become by the beginning of the nineteenth century, and in the 1740s almost the entire population lived on farms or in villages; and the few big cities (e.g., Boston, New York, Philadelphia, Charleston, Baltimore, Newport) were not *very* big. The second Awakening took place in a country that had expanded greatly and was expanding rapidly every day: villages were becoming towns, and towns were becoming cities, and most of the older cities (Newport and Charleston were exceptions) were well on their way to becoming very big cities. The first Awakening had been an exclusively rural phenomenon; the second, while mostly rural, also took place in urban places.

When the Reverend Timothy Dwight (1752–1817), a grandson of Jonathan Edwards, became president of Yale College in 1795, a post he continued to occupy until his death, he was distressed to discover that many students were reading, and were being very much influenced by, skeptical and deistic writers. In the next few years, through sermons and lectures, Dwight did battle—effective battle—against undergraduate infidelity. Soon orthodoxy once again prevailed on campus. In the fall of 1797 Dwight delivered an address to Yale bachelor's degree candidates titled "The Nature and Danger of Infidel Philosophy." The following year this address was published as a small book, a book that contributed to the beginning of the Second Great Awakening.

The Reverend Lyman Beecher (1775–1863), who had studied under Timothy Dwight at Yale, was the father of thirteen children (nine by his first wife, four by his second)—including Harriet Beecher Stowe, author of *Uncle Tom's Cabin*, and Henry Ward Beecher, probably America's most well-known Protestant minister in the second half of the nineteenth century. After having served for twelve years as a minister on Long Island and later for sixteen years as a minister in Litchfield, Connecticut, Beecher, a Calvinist, was called to a ministry in Boston, where the new theology of Unitarianism was proving to be more popular than Calvinism, the traditional theology of the Congregational churches of New England. From 1826 to 1832 Beecher, preaching from a Congregational pulpit in Boston, denounced Unitarianism and did his best to stop the exodus of Bostonians from the Congregational churches. It was in the course of this campaign—a losing campaign as it turned out, since Calvinism and even Arminianism continued to lose ground to Unitarianism—that Beecher became the best-known of all anti-Unitarian preachers. After this he was called to head a new Calvinist seminary in Cincinnati, the "metropolis of the West." It was in Cincinnati, situated just across the Ohio River from Kentucky, that his daughter Harriet first became acquainted with the American slavery that she so significantly helped to challenge with her famous novel.

Probably the most famous preacher of the Second Awakening was Charles Grandison Finney (1792–1875). Born in Connecticut but raised in Jefferson County, New York, Finney did not attend either college or a seminary. He became a lawyer, and then one day in his twenties he had a sudden conversion experience, after which he devoted himself to preaching and the study of theology. Later, after he had become a famous revivalist, he became a professor at Oberlin College in Ohio and eventually became president of the college—somewhat reminiscent of how a great revivalist of the original Great Awakening, Jonathan Edwards, had become president of the College of New Jersey (that is to say, Princeton).

In theology Finney was an Arminian, not a Calvinist; that is, he believed that humans, while sinful from birth, could overcome their sinfulness by freely accepting the saving grace that God offers to all men. Further, he believed that effective preaching, preaching that managed deeply to touch the hearts and minds of persons in the congregation, was an important means for provoking the individual person to accept the grace that God was offering him or her. God's grace was always being offered, since God wanted all persons to be saved; and all the individual had to do to become a saint was to accept the offer. Many persons never made the move needed to accept the offer, thereby assuring themselves of an eternity in hell. But if you were fortunate enough to hear the voice of a great preacher—a preacher of Finney's quality—there was a good chance that you would cease to resist God's offer, that you would accept the offer, thereby assuring yourself of an eternity in heaven. According to the Calvinist way of thinking, the move to accept God's offer of saving grace is inspired by God's grace. According to the Arminian/Finney way of thinking, the move to accept God's saving grade is often (though not always) inspired by great preaching.

And so Finney often held mass meetings, usually in rural settings but sometimes in cities. These were called "revivals," attended by hundreds and sometime thousands of persons. They abounded in religious excitement and enthusiasm, and, thanks to the collaboration between Finney and the Holy Ghost, they produced over many years a tremendous number of conversions. Although Finney was the most famous of all revivalists, his work was replicated by many lesser revivalists.

The revival work that Finney did in the decades preceding the Civil War was replicated by Billy Sunday in the early years of the twentieth century and by Billy Graham in the post-World War II years of the century. Finney, Sunday, Graham, and their many revivalist imitators kept alive throughout the nineteenth, twentieth, and early twenty-first century the old Protestant Consensus despite all liberal Protestant attempts to destroy it.

7

Transcendentalism

IN THIS CHAPTER WE return to the story of liberal Protestantism by discussing transcendentalism—a kind of "Protestantism" that was so liberal that many of its adherents didn't even pretend to be Christian.

The transcendentalist movement[1]—a movement of the 1830s and following decades that included such notable personages as Ralph Waldo Emerson, Henry David Thoreau, Margaret Fuller, Theodore Parker, Orestes Brownson, Bronson Alcott,[2] and Nathaniel Hawthorne[3]—was an offshoot of Unitarianism. Some of the early transcendentalists, however, later defected from the movement:

1. The indispensable book for anybody wishing to be acquainted with the movement is *The Transcendentalists*, an anthology edited by the great historian of early New England religion, Perry Miller. Another fine anthology is *The American Transcendentalists: Essential Writings*, edited by Lawrence Buell.

2. The father of Louisa May Alcott, author of *Little Women*.

3. Nathaniel Hawthorne was a friend of many transcendentalists, so much so that he briefly participated in their Brook Farm experiment, and one is tempted to count him as one of them. But the preoccupation with sin that he showed in his writings, both his novels and his short stories, indicates that he was not a true transcendentalist; for transcendentalists didn't dwell on the sinfulness of man, they dwelt on his potential divinity. If anything, Hawthorne's preoccupation with sin shows that he was an anti-transcendentalist.

Brownson became a Catholic, and Hawthorne (to judge from his many "dark" stories) obviously didn't agree with the common transcendentalist notion that humans are godlike beings. Like Unitarianism, it was a Boston-area movement, though its actual center was a Boston suburb, Concord, for it was there that the movement's most important figure, Emerson ("the Sage of Concord"), lived. Thoreau, Alcott, and (for a while) Hawthorne also lived in Concord. Today Emerson, Thoreau, Hawthorne, and the Alcotts are buried near one another at "Authors Ridge" in Concord's Sleepy Hollow Cemetery—a site well worth visiting by students of American history or American religion or American literature.

The intellectual parentage of transcendentalism was twofold: on the one hand, Unitarianism, especially as this was formulated and expressed by William Ellery Channing; on the other, German philosophy, as transmitted and explained to the English-speaking world by Samuel Taylor Coleridge (1772–1834) and Thomas Carlyle (1795–1881). Channing and his associates among the early Unitarians had taught Emerson and others that it was quite permissible to find fault with Christian doctrine while in pursuit of religious truth; and the lesson these latter learned was that it was even permissible to find fault with Unitarian doctrine. German philosophy (as filtered through Coleridge and Carlyle) had taught the transcendentalists the all-important distinction between reason and understanding.

The German theory of knowledge—which involved a great distinction between reason and understanding—involved a rejection of John Locke's theory of knowledge, which up to the 1830s had been the taken-for-granted American theory of knowledge; the Lockean theory was, for example, Thomas Jefferson's theory of knowledge and Channing's theory of knowledge. Locke held that all human knowledge is based on experience, either experience of the external (extra-mental) world through the five senses or experience of our own minds and their contents (sensations and feelings and thoughts) through reflection. There is no such thing as innate or inborn knowledge. When we come into the world, our mind is a *tabula rasa* (blank slate), waiting for experience to write upon it. German philosophers (Kant, Jacobi, Fichte, and Schelling) disagreed with Locke, arguing that at least some part of our knowledge is based on pre-experiential ideas: *innate* or *a priori* ideas.

Thus there are two kinds of knowledge according to the transcendentalists, who were in agreement with the German philosophers. Reason is the higher kind of knowledge, understanding the lower kind. Reason gives us intuitive knowledge (that is, an immediate knowledge that does not need to be proven, for it is self-evident) of the most important truths—truths about God, freedom of the will, immortality, and the laws of morality. Understanding gives us knowledge of ordinary things, knowledge of the material/sensual world that surrounds us. The knowledge given by reason is the knowledge that true religion and true philosophy are based on. The knowledge given by understanding is the knowledge upon which science, technology, commerce, and everyday mundane activities are based.

The early Unitarians (Channing et al.) were disciples of Locke, not of the Germans. And so when they tried to prove the truth of Christianity (that is, Christianity in its Unitarian form), they did so the way Locke would have done if had he been a Unitarian.[4] They didn't use innate knowledge; for as they (and Locke) saw it, there is no such thing as innate knowledge. They used only empirical facts and the reasonable inferences that can be drawn from these facts. To show that God exists, then, we begin with the fact of the universe and then draw the reasonable inference that such an immense and complex universe could only have been caused by a supreme being who is stupendously intelligent and powerful; in other words, God. And to show that Jesus was a being sent by God and that his teachings are true, we begin with the facts presented in the four Gospels. It is the miracles of the Gospels that prove that Jesus was sent from God and that his teachings are true. Only

---

4. And in fact Locke did offer a proof of a more or less orthodox form of Christianity in his book, *The Reasonableness of Christianity as Delivered in the Scriptures* (first published in 1695).

God can make a miracle, and why would God make the miracles of Jesus except to prove to us that Jesus, though not himself God, had a divine mission? The miracles connected with Jesus—e.g., the virgin birth, the resurrection, the loaves and fishes, the raising of Lazarus, the cures of lepers and blind men, and so on—are proofs (so argued the Unitarians) that Jesus was sent by God and spoke the truth; and therefore we can believe everything Jesus taught.

But this line of argument assumes that the facts presented in the four Gospels are truly facts. It assumes that the writers of the Gospels did not lie, did not exaggerate, did not make mistakes. It assumes that the writers of the four Gospels were either themselves eye-witnesses and ear-witnesses of Jesus or had access to reliable reports from those who were themselves eye-witnesses or ear-witnesses. And it assumes that the texts of the Gospels we have today are solidly based on original texts from the first century AD; no substantial mistakes by copyists, and no editorial amendments.

But any of this can be questioned—and *had* been questioned. It had been questioned, for instance, by David Hume in his essay on miracles; it had been questioned by Voltaire in his *Philosophical Dictionary*; and more and more it was being questioned by German scholars engaged in the "higher criticism" of the Bible.

To the transcendentalists (Emerson and company) it seemed absurd that the great and fundamental truths of religion—that God exists, that the human will is free, that there is a moral law by which we must live, that the soul is immortal—should be trusted to the fragile bark of Locke-style proof. Suppose it can be shown that the Gospels are not totally reliable historical documents—poof! There goes our religion! We must thereafter live in doubt. How can we prevent this doubt? Did the transcendentalists have an answer? Yes. First, they said, we recognize that the Locke-style argument is an argument that comes from the understanding, our lower form of knowledge. Next, we turn instead to reason, our higher form of knowledge. Reason assures us, not just of the probability, but of the *certainty*, of the fundamental principles of religion: God, freedom, immortality, and the moral law. We accept the teachings of Jesus, not because *he* taught them, but because they tally with what reasons tells us.

A great battle between transcendentalists (whose ranks included many "advanced" or "progressive" Unitarians) and conventional Unitarians took place over the issue of miracles. The older Unitarians insisted that belief in the Gospel miracles is essential to Christianity. The transcendentalists didn't deny the miracles so much as they said that they are irrelevant. Who cares if Jesus was born of a virgin? Who cares if he used the precise words attributed to him in the Gospels? Who cares if he rose from the dead? We have an innate and intuitive knowledge of the fundamental truths of religion. We don't need miracles to prove these truths to us. We don't believe these truths because Jesus told them to us. We believe them because we *see* that they are true. We know that Jesus was a representative of God not because Jesus worked miracles, but because he saw these great fundamental truths as clearly as, or more clearly than, any man has ever seen them. Though Jesus Christ was a great man, a truly God-inspired man, we need not take the great truths of religion from him; we can intuit them for ourselves. Jesus doesn't *teach* us what we don't know; he *reminds* us of what we do know.

And what do we know? Not just that God exists, and not just that we are immortal souls, and not just that the good life is the life or moral goodness. But also that we humans are godlike beings, that in the last analysis there is no ontological gap between us and God, that deep down we are one with God, that we are parts or aspects of the divine foundation of reality.

ے॰ ॰ؤ

The great gap between the Unitarian view of religion and the transcendentalist view was first clearly, indeed shockingly, brought out in Emerson's "Divinity School Address" of July 15, 1838.[5] This was a commencement speech delivered to the graduating class

5. For a small but essential section of this address, see Miller, *The Transcendentalists*, 192. For an unabridged version see any of a number of collections of Emerson's essays, for instance: Buell, *American Transcendentalists*, 129–45; or Ziff, *Ralph Waldo Emerson: Selected Essays*, 107–28.

of Harvard's School of Divinity, which was in effect a seminary for Unitarian ministers; the men in the graduating class would soon be called to be pastors in Unitarian churches. Emerson, who himself had graduated from Harvard and had been a Unitarian minister until a few years earlier, shocked the older generation of Unitarians by saying things like these below.

- "Truly speaking, it is not instruction, but provocation, that I can receive from another soul. What he announces, I must find true in me, or reject; and on his word, or as his second, be he who he may, I can accept nothing."

- "There is no doctrine of the Reason that will bear to be taught by the Understanding."

- "The word 'Miracle,' as pronounced by Christian churches, gives a false impression; it is Monster. It is not one with the blowing clover and the falling rain."

- "[Historical Christianity] has dwelt, it dwells, with noxious exaggeration about the *person* of Jesus."

- "But by this eastern monarchy of a Christianity, which indolence and fear have built, the friend of man is made the injurer of man."

- "That which shows God in me, fortifies me. That which shows God out of me, makes me a wart and a wen."

- "Men have come to speak of the revelation as somewhat long ago given and done, as if God were dead."

- "The faith should blend with the light of rising and of setting suns, with the flying cloud, the singing bird, and the breath of flowers. But now the priest's Sabbath has lost the Splendor of nature; it is unlovely."

- "The true Christianity—a faith like Christ's in the infinitude of man—is lost. None believeth in the soul of man, but only in some man or person old and departed."

- "[Men] think society wiser than their soul, and know not that one soul, and their soul, is wiser than the whole world."

- "Yourself a newborn bard of the Holy Ghost, cast behind you all conformity, and acquaint men at first hand with Deity."

Andrews Norton—formerly a professor at the Divinity School, who was spoken of by some people as "the pope of Unitarianism," and who had been one of Emerson's teachers at Harvard's School of Divinity—replied to Emerson with a lecture delivered almost a year to the day after Emerson's scandalous speech. Norton's attempted rebuttal was later published as a pamphlet titled "The Latest Form of Infidelity."[6] Norton believed that everything hinged on the miracles of Jesus. If there were no miracles, we have no reason to believe that Jesus was sent by God and no reason to believe the truths spoken by Jesus. Norton was one of the older generation of Unitarians who believed—foolishly, as it turned out—that you could chop off some branches from the tree of Christian orthodoxy without this leading to the chopping off of more and more branches by the next generation. His rebuttal did little to hinder the progress of transcendentalism.

Of course, what the transcendentalists saw as the fundamental truths of religion are not specifically Christian truths; they were seen by the transcendentalists as fundamental to *any* sound religion. If so, this means that all religions, or at least all "higher" religions (e.g., Christianity, Judaism, Islam, Hinduism, Buddhism) are more or less equal. Transcendentalists recognized this and had open-minded attitudes toward religions other than Christianity. Most transcendentalists, it is true, retained a special affection for Christianity above all other religions, and for Jesus above all other prophets. But nothing in their theory compelled them to do so. These pro-Christian preferences were residues from the Unitarian Christianity of their younger days.

For the transcendentalists, the existence of God is a self-evident truth—but it is not self-evident that God is a *personal* God. Emerson himself thought of God as impersonal, though he had no objection

6. See Norton, "A Discourse on the Latest Form of Infidelity."

if others, in certain moments of exaltation, think of God as personal. And so are the laws of morality self-evident truths. And so is the immortal and godlike nature of the human soul a self-evident truth. We are all aware of these truths. At least we are *potentially* aware; and if it were not for certain factors that blind us for the moment, we would all be *actually* aware of these truths. And what are the factors that blind us? Answer: the ordinary business of the world—for example, politics, getting and spending money, trying to keep the respect and goodwill of our neighbors by conforming to their prejudices, and so on. If we could, at least for a moment, disregard these factors and look into the depths of our souls, we'd see that we are all rooted in God, that we are all parts of God, that we are all in the last analysis divine beings. The Bible is a good book, but we don't need the Bible to know the most important things. All we have to do is to look deep inside ourselves. That's where Jesus looked, and it was out of his own depths that he produced his wise sayings and led his godlike life. We can do the same.[7]

☙ ❧

Theodore Parker (1810–60) was a Unitarian minister who, while embracing transcendentalist ideas, did not resign from the Unitarian ministry. In this he was unlike two other transcendentalists, Emerson and George Ripley, both of whom abandoned the ministry and Unitarianism itself when they realized that Unitarian orthodoxy was not compatible with their new ideas. Not so Parker. He hoped that he might carry Unitarianism itself in a transcendentalist direction. But his more "advanced" views were too shocking for the great majority of his Unitarian fellow-ministers, and they tried to subject him to a de facto excommunication by "shunning" him; that is, by the refusal to exchange pulpits with him. Did this drive Parker out of the Unitarian fold? Far from it. His supporters, who were numerous, created a new congregation that met every

---

7. For Emerson's best expressions of these views, see his essays "Self-reliance," "The Oversoul," and "The Divinity School Address," as well as his poem "The Problem."

Sunday in a large theater on Tremont Street, Boston. This soon became the single largest Unitarian congregation in New England.

In his famous sermon of 1841, "A Discourse of the Transient and Permanent in Christianity," Parker created the template subsequently used by all liberal Protestants down to the present day. According to this template we need to go through a two-step process if we (liberal Protestants) wish to remain Christians while rejecting portions, even very large portions, of traditional Christian doctrine. First, we must distinguish between those features of Christianity that are *essential* and those that are merely *incidental*. Second, we must discard the incidental features if in our best judgment they need to be rejected, while retaining the essential features. And hence our new system of belief and practice will still be Christianity, and we will still be Christians.

Parker's idea was that the essential or permanent beliefs of Christianity are few and easy to understand: (1) that God exists; (2) that our moral duty is summed up in the commandment that we must love our neighbors; and (3) that our souls survive the death of the body. All other beliefs are incidental, and may be discarded if they no longer suit the times we happen to be living in.

Almost—but not quite—as essential is that Christianity must focus on the life and teachings of Jesus Christ, that young Jewish prophet of the first century who more than anybody else (to date) exhibited as a model the mind and character of God. For

> if it could be proved—as it cannot—in opposition to the greatest amount of historical evidence ever collected on any similar point, that the Gospels were the fabrication of designing and artful men, that Jesus of Nazareth had never lived, still Christianity would stand firm, and fear no evil. None of the doctrines of that religion would fall to the ground; for, if true, they stand by themselves.[8]

The text Parker chose for this famous sermon is a verse from Luke: "Heaven and earth shall pass away; but my words shall not pass away" (Luke 21:33) The long history of Christianity, Parker says, is the history of ever-changing ceremonial forms and

8. Parker, "Discourse of the Transient and Permanent in Christianity," 272.

ever-changing doctrines. The ceremonies and doctrines that seem just right for expressing the essential truths of Christianity in one age no longer seem appropriate in the next age; and so they have been changed and will be further changed in following ages. But this doesn't mean that Christianity itself changes. These changing forms and doctrines are attempts, never perfectly successful, to express the unchanging essence of Christianity.

Parker made a further distinction that became stock in trade for all subsequent liberal Christians, a distinction between religion and theology. True Christianity is religion; theology is a theory *about* religion. The religion is unchanging—just as the stars are unchanging. Theology has undergone many changes—just as astronomy, the theory about the stars, has undergone many changes. Let us hold on to the permanent thing, Christianity. And let us bid goodbye to the transient thing, our current theology whatever it may be, when we can find a better.

It isn't the Bible—that far-from-infallible collection of books—that teaches us the essential truths of Christianity. It isn't even Jesus, that godlike man, who teaches us these essential truths. How then do we know them? Parker, while he doesn't explicitly spell it out in his famous sermon, takes for granted what Emerson and other transcendentalists took for granted, namely the distinction between reason and understanding. Reason, that higher power of knowledge, gives us an intuitive knowledge of higher truths, those truths of religion generally and of the best of all religions, Christianity. The Bible in its best parts *reminds* us of these things, things we already know apart from the Bible. And Jesus by his life and teachings is the very best reminder the world has ever seen of these intuitively known truths.[9]

I have said earlier that that liberal Protestants usually give morality a central and very emphatic place in their idea of Christianity; and that the morality of the liberal Protestant often goes beyond the

---

9. This paragraph summarizes briefly—all too briefly and without a hundred nuances—an argument Parker presents at considerable length in a posthumously published 335-page book, *A Discourse on Matters Pertaining to Religion.*

morality emphasized by more traditional Protestants. It is as if by doubling down on the moral element of Christianity they can make up for their "softness" on the doctrinal element. This is strikingly true in the case of Parker. He burned with moral indignation against slavery. He spoke against it not only to his Boston congregation but to tens of thousands of others, regardless of their religion or non-religion, as he traveled by train around much of the Northeastern quadrant of the USA. It is said that Lincoln himself once heard Parker speak against slavery when Parker paid a visit to Illinois.

It should be noted, however, that anti-slavery Protestantism was not limited to liberal Protestants. Far from it. The abolition movement was created and sustained mainly by traditional Protestants. The difference with regard to slavery was that virtually all liberal Protestants were anti-slavery while only a minority of traditionalists were. And in the South, of course, almost all traditional Protestants were pro-slavery.

Before closing this chapter, let me note that it pains me to have to class Emerson among the wreckers of American Christianity. For I personally have tremendous admiration for Emerson—as a writer, a thinker, a religious (albeit non-Christian) hero, and a great and good man. All the same, his transcendentalism was an important step in the dissolution of American Protestant Christianity. His pantheistic naturalism easily led to non-theistic (atheistic) naturalism.

In only a generation, then, beginning with Channing and ending with Emerson and his friends, had Boston Protestantism evolved (or devolved, if you prefer) from the liberal religion of Unitarianism to the ultra-liberal religion of transcendentalism. And from transcendentalism, despite all its spirituality, it was but a short step to naturalism; that is to say, atheism.

8

The Second Assault

Agnosticism

APART FROM THE UNITARIANS and the transcendentalists, who, for all their tremendous long-run importance, were no more than a small fraction of the American population in the days prior to the Civil War (1861–65), the Protestant Consensus remained intact among almost all American Protestants for the first two-thirds of the nineteenth century. Beginning, however, in the decades just after the Civil War, American Protestantism was confronted by a powerful anti-Christianity intellectual movement which we may call "agnosticism."[1] The agnostic movement was made up of three components:

- Agnosticism proper, or the agnostic theory of knowledge.
- Darwinism.
- The "higher criticism" of the Bible, mostly a German phenomenon.

---

1. To remind the reader of what I have said earlier, this was the second of three great attacks on Christianity; the first being deism, the third being the sexual revolution.

In England this agnostic attack on Christianity produced what may be called "the mid-Victorian religious crisis," and in America it produced what may be called "the post-Civil War religious crisis."

I will here use the word "agnosticism" in two ways: in a narrow sense to refer to the agnostic theory of knowledge, and in a broader sense to refer to the late nineteenth century anti-Christianity movement as a whole.

As a theory of knowledge *agnosticism* holds that it is impossible to know whether God exists or does not exist. This theory was not a thing of American provenance; it was an English import to America. The United States had gained its political independence from Britain in the latter part of the 1700s, but by the latter part of the 1800s it had not yet gained its intellectual independence; it was still heavily dependent on England for its new and fashionable ideas. Intellectual independence didn't come until the twentieth century.

On the European continent, especially in Germany, many leading anti-Christian intellectuals (e.g., Feuerbach, Schopenhauer, Marx) had already moved on to atheism. But England was intellectually more conservative; and in England religion was too respectable a thing, even among nonbelievers, for any significant part of the public to support and endorse outright atheism. And so anti-Christianity in England usually stopped, at least for the moment, at agnosticism.

It was a new word, by the way—this "agnosticism." It was coined by one of the chief English Victorian anti-Christians, the philosopher-biologist Thomas Henry Huxley, who because of his vigorous defense of Charles Darwin's theory of evolution earned the nickname "Darwin's bulldog." Hitherto the word for what came to be called "agnosticism" had been "skepticism." And thus David Hume, the famous eighteenth-century Scottish philosopher (about whom, by the way, Huxley had written a short biography in the British Men of Letters series) had been labeled a skeptic. But one can be skeptical about many things—about the existence of God, yes; but also about the traditional account of the career of Richard III, or about the Weather Bureau's forecast that it will snow tomorrow, or about a thousand other things. The great advantage of the word "agnosticism" was its specificity; it referred precisely and exclusively to skepticism as to the existence of God. When you heard a man say, "I am an agnostic," you knew exactly what the object of his particular kind of skepticism was.[2] The word, invented in 1869, was derived from the Greek word *gnosis* (one of a number of Greek words for knowledge) plus the Greek negative prefix *a-*, equivalent to "un" or "non" in English.

There were some *Christian* agnostics, that is, Christian apologists who argued (a) that agnosticism showed that nobody can prove the *non*-existence of God, and (b) that therefore we are free to *believe* in God's existence, to have *faith* in the existence of God. The most notable of these Christian agnostics was Henry Longueville Mansel (1820–71), an Anglican priest, a professor at the University of Oxford, and in the last years of his life the Dean of St. Paul's Cathedral in London. The best-known expression of his Christian agnosticism can be found in his book *The Limits of Religious Thought* (1858).[3] However, despite Mansel and a few others, agnosticism was a predominantly *anti*-Christianity phenomenon. The typical agnostic, both in England and in America, had little or no use for Christianity.

The leading English agnostic was the philosopher and polymath Herbert Spencer (1820–1903), according to whom all of reality can be divided into two parts, the knowable and the unknowable. (Note well: the *unknowable*, not the *unknown*.) Many things are unknown today that will be known tomorrow (e.g., who will win the baseball world series in the year 2025, or whether there are

---

2. Nowadays, however, this advantage has largely been lost, as many people (linguistically careless people) use the word "agnostic" as a synonym for "doubtful" or "undecided." As in: "I am agnostic on the question of whether or not aluminum bats should be allowed in professional baseball."

3. This book was re-issued in 2018 by Forgotten Books.

human-type beings living on planets surrounding distant stars), and many things that are in principle knowable will very probably never actually be known because doing the required research is either too much trouble or too expensive or not worth our time. For example, in all probability we will never have an exact answer to the question, "What is the number of mosquitoes in Pennsylvania?" Of course there is a correct answer to the question, and God—if God exists—knows that answer. But so what? Who cares? However, there are some things, according to Spencer, which, given the nature of these things and the limits of the human power of knowledge, cannot *possibly* be known. What we humans can know is reality insofar as it presents itself to our senses—not just our naked senses but our senses aided by microscopes, telescopes, and other technological enhancements. In short, we can know the *appearances* of things. And we can know as-yet-hidden appearances that can reasonably be inferred from these sense appearances. But we cannot know the non-apparent or non-sensible reality that lies behind—or underlies, or causes—all appearances. We cannot, in short, know ultimate realities. We can know more and more about the world of appearances, but we can never know the deeper reality itself.

But we can *guess* about reality. And we can *mythologize* about it. Religious people may guess that the ultimate reality is God or gods. Non-religious people may guess that the ultimate reality is some mindless "stuff." But neither can ever *know* what the ultimate reality is. They can only guess. And their guesses can never be verified or falsified. Spencer had no objection to religious belief (though he was not himself a believer). But the believer should remind himself or herself that this belief is simply that—*belief*, not knowledge.

There were other prominent agnostics in Victorian England: for instance, Thomas Henry Huxley, Leslie Stephen (the father of Virginia Wolff), and William Kingdom Clifford (against whom William James did battle in his famous essay "The Will to Believe"). No doubt the best-known English agnostic of the day was Charles Darwin, author of *The Origin of Species* (1859). Darwin, however, unlike Spencer, Huxley, Stephen, and Clifford, was not a pro-agnosticism propagandist. He just happened to be doubtful as to the existence of God. He didn't shout his agnosticism from Victorian rooftops. He did not publicly recommend it to the world at large. And he did not consider his *The Origin of Species* to be an argument in favor of agnosticism—though many agnostics *did* consider it to be such. Darwin's agnosticism appears to have had little direct connection with his famous book. It didn't inspire the book, though it may have been to some degree the result of the book. In his youth, prior to his voyage on the *Beagle*, he was a Christian believer and he intended to become a clergyman in the Church of England. As years went by, however, his Christian faith dwindled, and by the time he was in his fifties or sixties it had turned to dust.

In America, while there were some conspicuous agnostics, none of them was of the intellectual stature of Huxley, Spencer, or Leslie Stephen. The two best-known American agnostics were Robert Ingersoll (1833–1899), sometimes called "the Great Agnostic," an intellectual lightweight but a talented orator in the days when grandiloquent public speaking had not yet ceased to be fashionable; and Clarence Darrow (1857–1938), the county's most famous criminal defense lawyer, best-known for his appearance at the 1925 "monkey trial" in Dayton, Tennessee. For serious pro-agnosticism arguments, Americans had to depend on English thinkers.

The agnostics had allies who, perhaps unwittingly and even perhaps unwillingly, provided them with further anti-Christian ammunition. In particular, there were two important allies, the Darwinian evolutionists and the German Bible critics.

ல ல

Darwinism, the theory of biological evolution by means of random mutation and natural selection, was introduced to the world with the 1859 publication of Charles Darwin's landmark book, *The Origin of Species*,[4] and it proved to be a great help in promoting the

---

4. The theory was independently discovered by another English naturalist, Alfred Russel Wallace (1823–1913). Darwin, it seems, had discovered the theory many years before Wallace, but had not published his discovery. It was

anti-Christianity of the agnostic movement even though this was certainly not the author's intention.

How did Darwinism have an anti-Christianity impact?

For one thing, if Darwin was right, the account of creation given in the first book of the Bible, the Book of Genesis, was wrong, phenomenally wrong, and it was wrong in at least two ways. First, a literal reading of Genesis puts the creation of the world at a date about six thousand years ago. But Darwin's gradual evolution of countless living things could not possibly have occurred in a mere six thousand years. At least hundreds of millions of years would have been required, if not more. Second, Genesis says, or at least clearly seems to imply, that species are fixed; they don't evolve into or out of other species. According to a literal reading of Genesis, wolves today, for instance, are the same as they were at the moment of their creation six thousand years ago. But according to Darwin, today's wolves evolved from pre-wolves, and these pre-wolves evolved from pre-pre-wolves, and so on all the way back to the most primitive of all life forms.

Now if we accept Darwin and reject the Bible's account of the beginning of the world and the beginning of living things, that means we think that the Book of Genesis is seriously mistaken. But if Genesis is wrong, how can we have confidence in other books of the Bible? If the Bible is not infallible in Genesis, how can it be infallible elsewhere? If the Bible is a God-made book (as Christians believe), how can Genesis be mistaken? And not just a little bit mistaken but grossly mistaken. Darwinism and the Bible, it seemed, were plainly incompatible with one another.

Many Protestants tried to get around this difficulty by arguing that there is no need to read Genesis *literally*. It should be read not as history or science but as poetry. Its facts cannot be contradicted by science because its "facts" were not meant by the author (or authors) of Genesis to be scientific or historical facts.

announced to the scientific world by both Darwin and Wallace on July 1, 1858, at a meeting of the Linnean Society of London. The theory has always been called Darwinism, not Wallaceism, even by Wallace himself. I suppose this is for two reasons: that Darwin came up with the theory earlier than Wallace, and that Darwin soon published his big world-famous book.

They were intended as symbols; they are metaphors; in any case they don't mean what they seem to mean at first glance. They tell a story, but it is not a scientific or historical story; it is a moral and religious story. The reader should extract the solid religious-moral kernel while paying little attention to the brightly colored pseudo-scientific and pseudohistorical shell it is encased in. And so we can say that Darwin is compatible with the Bible provided the latter is understood in the right way.

Even this, however, wasn't good enough to evade the anti-Christianity effect of Darwinism. The Christian might be willing to accept the Darwinian story of the long and very gradual evolution of living things—until the Christian notices that it's a Godless evolution. The Genesis story, even when read as poetry, represents God as actually creating things. But God is absent in the Darwinian story. Evolution happens on its own by means of random mutation and natural selection. God does not intervene. God does not need to intervene. Isn't the Darwinian theory, then, an atheistic theory? That was the answer given by Charles Hodge in a small book he wrote in 1874. Hodge, a professor at Princeton Theological Seminary, was the leading Presbyterian (and Calvinist) theologian of his day in the United States. The book in question was titled *What is Darwinism?* In the last page or two of the book Hodge gives his answer to the question expressed in the title. "We have thus arrived at the answer to our question, What is Darwinism? It is atheism." Hodge quickly adds that this is not to say "that Mr. Darwin himself and all who adopt his views are atheists; but it means that his theory itself is atheistic; that the exclusion of design from nature . . . is tantamount to atheism."[5]

If you were an anti-Christianity agnostic, Darwinism provided your intellectual cannons with lots of ammunition to fire at the walls of Christianity. And not many agnostics failed to take advantage of the great supply of Darwinian ammunition. See especially the writings of Thomas Henry Huxley.

5. Hodge, *What is Darwinism?*, 156–57.

German Bible critics, practitioners of the so-called "higher criticism" of the Bible, had been undermining confidence in the reliability of the Bible since late in the 1700s.[6] They did not all agree among themselves, and often wrote books and articles proving that one or another was mistaken about this or that. But they were generally agreed on certain skeptical points regarding the Bible:

- That the traditional authorships of many books of the Bible were mistaken (e.g., Moses did not write the first five books of the OT, David did not write the entire Book of Psalms, Solomon did not write Proverbs, Isaiah did not write all three parts of the Book of Isaiah).

- That the history of Israel given in the OT was at best only semi-accurate; it contained many errors.

- That the authorship of some NT books was uncertain.

- That the accounts given in the four canonical Gospels of the deeds and sayings of Jesus were not fully reliable.

- That the fourth Gospel was a doubtful thing with regard both to its authorship and its content.

All this posed difficulties for both Protestants and Catholics, but more so for Protestants than for Catholics. Catholics held that the ultimate authority in religion was the Church itself, not the Bible. According to the Catholic view, it was the Church that had produced the Bible; and if there was any question as to the correct interpretation of the Bible, it was the Catholic Church—the actual church headquartered in Rome and headed by the Pope—that could provide the correct interpretation. If the Bible seemed to be defective in any way, that was alarming but not devastating; for the alarmed Catholic could rely on his Church to make good any apparent defects in the Bible. But for Protestants any defect in the Bible was earth-shaking. For (according to old Protestant sayings)

---

6. There were of course some non-German critics, the best-known of whom was the Frenchman Ernest Renan (1823–92), who wrote a famous/notorious *Life of Jesus* (1863). But the higher criticism was mainly a German thing.

"the Bible is the religion of Protestants"—"the Bible, the whole Bible, and nothing but the Bible."

Many (though not all) of the German critics had no intention of undermining or destroying Christianity. Their aim was simply to make Christianity more scientifically and historically reliable. Of course their criticism was a departure from traditional Christian belief, both Protestant and Catholic; a departure in the direction of liberal Christianity; that is, a departure in the direction of an unorthodox and watered-down Christianity. Still, they *intended* to preserve Christianity, at least Protestant Christianity—but a *modern* Protestantism that was willing to accept the methods and the findings of modern science and historiography.

The late-nineteenth-century anti-Christianity movement (that is, the agnosticism movement) was happy to embrace this German criticism, for it provided the movement with further ammunition to be used against Christianity. Not only was it impossible, as the agnostic theory of knowledge said, to obtain knowledge of God by means of human reason; but a supposed alternative source of knowledge about God, divine revelation as found in the Bible, had been shown by the German critics to be a very doubtful thing.

How did American Protestants respond to the agnosticism attack on their religion? They had two quite opposite responses, modernism and fundamentalism, as we'll see in the next few chapters.

9

Modernism

The Liberal Response to Agnosticism

IN THE DECADES FOLLOWING the rise and very limited spread of
Unitarianism and transcendentalism, the vast majority of American Protestants remained theologically conservative. That is to say,
they adhered to the articles of what I have called the Protestant
Consensus. But something of a division could be observed among
this vast majority; not a division in doctrine, but a division in religious style. It was a division between those who sympathized with
a strongly emotional style of revivalism and those who did not.
This division in style went all the way back to the Great Awakening
of the 1740s. The leaders of the first Awakening (e.g., John Wesley,
George Whitefield, Jonathan Edwards) regarded the strong expression of religious emotion as the result of a great outpouring of
grace by the Holy Ghost. Unsympathetic ministers, who preferred
a religious style that was more "rational" and therefore less emotional, disagreed. One of them, Ezra Stiles (who eventually became
president of Yale College), summed up the attitude of the critics
when he complained that during the Awakening, "Multitudes were
seriously, soberly, and solemnly out of their wits."[1]

1. Miller and Heimert, *The Great Awakening*, 595.

During the revolutionary era, from the 1760s through the 1780s, religious emotionalism receded, to be replaced for the time being by political and patriotic emotionalism; but near the end of the century, the Revolution having been won and the new national republic launched, religious emotionalism made a return with what came to be called the Second Great Awakening. Consider the famous week-long revival that took place in August of 1801 at Cane Ridge in Kentucky, not far from Lexington. Peter Cartwright, who later became a notable revivalist, was present when a boy at Cane Ridge during the famous revival, and he gives a description of the event in his autobiography (first published in 1856). As Cartwright reported it,

> The mighty power of God was displayed in a very extraordinary manner; many were moved to tears, and bitter and loud crying for mercy . . . It was supposed that there were in attendance at times during the meeting from twelve to twenty-five thousand people. Hundreds fell prostrate under the mighty power of God, as men slain in battle . . . It was said, by truthful witnesses, that at times more than one thousand persons broke into loud shouting all at once, and that the shouts could be heard for miles around . . . I suppose since the day of Pentecost, there was hardly ever a greater revival of religion than at Cane Ridge.[2]

As had been the case with the First Awakening, many ministers and lay persons disapproved of the strong emotionalism of the Second Awakening. This disagreement was to a great degree an urban-versus-rural disagreement. Religious emotionalism tended to be approved of in the country, disapproved of in cities.

However, despite this significant disagreement in religious style, prior to the Civil War the Protestant Consensus held among almost all Protestants. There had been, it is true, something of a liberal-versus-conservative division from the beginning of the nineteenth century, with Unitarians and Universalists being on the liberal side of the divide, all other Protestants on the conservative

2. Cartwright, *Autobiography*, 33–35.

side. But the liberals were comparatively small in number; they were vastly outnumbered by the conservatives; and so they could be ignored by mainstream Protestants. It was not until the agnostic attack on Christianity that American Protestantism as a whole split into a large liberal section and a large conservative section.

Many Protestants, those of a liberal or "rational" temperament, in order to hold on to their religion in the face of the criticisms of Christianity made by agnostics and their allies, followed the pattern created by early Unitarianism. That is to say,

1. They conceded that there is much merit in the agnostic criticisms.

2. They argued that the critics, whatever their merits, went too far when they rejected Christianity altogether.

3. They then blended Christianity and the agnostic criticisms so as to create a "new and improved" version of Christianity—a liberal or modern version.

4. They argued that Christian morality is the essence of Christianity.

Let's take a closer look at each of these steps in the liberal reaction to the agnostic movement.

1. Liberal Christians conceded that there was much merit in the agnostic critique of Christianity. This meant that they were conceding that there was much merit in (a) agnosticism as a theory of knowledge, (b) the Darwinian theory of biological evolution, and (c) the higher criticism of the Bible. They made all three concessions by opting to be "modern" rather than pre-modern in their response to then-current fashions in philosophy, science, and scholarship. If, liberals argued, Christianity rejects agnosticism, Darwinism, and modern Biblical criticism, it will be telling modern men and women that Christianity is out of step with the great intellectual

progress that is characteristic of the modern world. Now it may be okay in the eyes of uneducated men and women to reject agnosticism, Darwinism, and modern biblical criticism—in other words, it may be okay in the eyes of persons who are perfectly content to live out of the mainstream of modern intellectual progress. For centuries most humans had been like that—intellectually backward. But that is no longer the case. Now, at least in America, many people get a high school education; more than a few even go on to college; and in the future secondary and higher education will be even more common than it is today. And it is these people, these educated people, who will be the social and cultural leaders of tomorrow. If Christianity is unable to keep up with the world's intellectual progress, these people, these social and cultural leaders, will have no choice but to abandon the old religion. Therefore we must accept the results of modern intellectual progress. To reject these results will be to allow Christianity to die out. So argued liberal Protestants.

2. But while they were willing to accept the results of modern intellectual progress in philosophy, science, and scholarship, liberal Protestants were quite unwilling to accept the agnostic demand that they abandon Christianity altogether. Why should they? After all, it was a marvelous worldview, far superior to the godless materialism that agnostics were offering as an alternative. Moreover, if it is progress that's wanted, what has contributed more to the progress of the human race than Christianity? It has been history's greatest source of moral progress, intellectual progress, social progress, and even material progress. Most important of all, Christianity is a *true* religion. The critiques made by the agnostic movement may puzzle us for a moment; but we know—we feel it in our very bones—that Christianity is true. We'd be crazy to give it up. So let's do both: let's accept the results of modern science and scholarship, and let's remain Christian.

3. Liberal Protestants, then, had to develop a "new and improved" version of Christianity, a version that would be a blend of the best of agnosticism and the best of old-fashioned Christianity. They would have to find a way of accepting the truths of the Old Testament, the New Testament, the Spencerian theory of knowledge, the Darwinian theory of evolution, and the higher criticism of the Bible—a way of accepting all these truths and blending them into a modernized version of the Christian religion, a new and better version.

4. The Social Gospel movement was a moral byproduct of post-Civil War American liberal Protestantism. Old-fashioned Protestants continued to stress old-fashioned Protestant moral virtues such as sobriety, chastity, honesty, thrift, and piety. But the Social Gospel Protestants, while not discarding—though perhaps slightly downgrading—the old-fashioned virtues, stressed the moral importance of contributing to social reform and betterment.

A hyper-liberal response to the agnostic movement came from the great Victorian poet and critic Matthew Arnold (1822–88) who, though an Englishman, was well-known and influential on this western side of the Atlantic. He was the son of Dr. Thomas Arnold (1795–1842), the famous Headmaster of Rugby School. Thomas Arnold was an ordained minister in the Church of England, and he was a great champion of the idea of "broad church" Anglicanism. He wanted a Church of England that was open to *all* English Protestants; and that meant a church that would de-emphasize those things that divided English Protestants and emphasize those things upon which all Protestants could agree. And what did all Protestants (except Unitarians and Universalists) agree on? The Bible, the Trinity, the incarnation, the atonement, the virgin birth, the resurrection, the Ten Commandments, the Sermon on the Mount, heaven and hell. They agreed on what I have been calling "the Protestant Consensus." Let's have a national church, Dr. Arnold argued, that will include everybody who believes in these basic and noncontroversial doctrines.

By the time his son Matthew began writing about religion, decades later, agnosticism and Darwinism and the higher criticism had appeared on the intellectual scene, and they had taken their toll in the Protestant world. The elder Arnold didn't have to deal with these things; but the younger Arnold, who like his father wanted the Church of England to be inclusive or "broad," couldn't avoid dealing with them. The younger Arnold thought that the agnostic triad of agnosticism-criticism-evolution had pretty much demolished traditional Christian doctrine; at least it had demolished it in the eyes of intelligent and educated men and women. But Matthew Arnold was unwilling to abandon Christianity; he was, after all, his father's son. Matthew wanted a church that was truly national; he wanted people to keep reading the Bible, if only for its poetic value;[3] he wanted people to keep going to church on Sundays; he wanted people to practice Christian morality. He thought these goals could be achieved by reducing the creed to a minimum that all Protestants could agree on; but unlike his father's creed, Matthew's would be a *very bare* minimum. Matthew's creed would discard all elements that any believer in God might find objectionable; only agnostics and outright atheists would object. And so Matthew Arnold made two strategic moves, two strategic redefinitions. (1) He redefined religion (by which he meant Christianity) as "morality touched by emotion." The essence of religion, then, is morality; that is, right conduct along with right emotion that would inspire that right conduct. This means that religion is in large measure an emotional thing, a thing of feeling or sentiment, not a thing having to do with *knowledge*. (2) He redefined God as "the eternal not-ourselves that makes for righteousness." In other words, there is some great power in existence (possibly a personal power, but not necessarily so) that is supportive of our efforts to be morally good. That's a minimal creed indeed; a far, far cry from

---

3. Arnold, one of the leading Victorian poets and perhaps the greatest of all Victorian critics of poetry, greatly overestimated the beneficial impact that poetry could have on the mind and heart of the average man or woman. See his famous essay "The Study of Poetry."

the classical creeds of Christianity, beginning with the Apostles' Creed, and a far, far cry from the traditional Protestant Consensus.

In the USA no liberal Protestant, no matter how liberal, went quite as far as Matthew Arnold in "saving" Christianity by getting rid of almost all its doctrinal content. But they all *tended* in the same direction. In a variety of ways they watered down the strong doctrinal content of classical Protestantism, and they showed that they were prepared to water it down even more if need be. At the same time liberal ministers usually concealed from the average lay person how far they had gone in their revision of doctrine. They did this by using traditional Christian rhetoric in the pulpit while (in their own minds) redefining the meaning of certain terms. (This doublespeak can still be found on Sundays in many liberal churches.) Keep in mind that Matthew Arnold was not a clergyman; he had secular sources of income; and thus he had no fear that he might be dismissed from a church post if suspected of heresy. In America, at least for many years until liberal beliefs began to "trickle down" to lay persons, liberal Protestantism was relatively common among ministers but rare among laypersons; and thus, when speaking or writing about liberal ideas, liberal ministers had to keep in mind the possibility of losing their jobs. One way of "playing it safe" was, when delivering a sermon, to use religious or Biblical expressions that could have two meanings: a liberal meaning in the mind of the up-to-date minister delivering the sermon, and a conservative or traditional meaning in the minds of the lay persons hearing the sermon.

The Agnostic Theory of Knowledge

According to the agnostic or Spencerian theory there can be no *knowledge* of God. For God, if he exists, does so in the realm of the unknowable. We humans are unable to know anything of the existence of God or of the nature of God.

Liberal Protestants had a number of ways of trying to get around this difficulty.

a. Some liberal Protestants granted, in agreement with agnostics, that we know the world via sense experience and the reasonable inferences that can be drawn from those sense experiences, and that neither sense experience nor the inferences drawn from it can lead to knowledge of God. However, they made one exception to the agnostic theory by postulating a faculty of knowledge that goes above and beyond sense experience, and they claimed that this extra-sensory faculty gives us direct awareness of God. This was an idea left over from transcendentalist days, reminiscent of the transcendentalist idea of reason (as opposed to understanding). A good example of this response was *The Religious Feeling, a Study for Faith*, by Newman Smyth (1877). This, however, was an implausible exception; for the days of transcendentalism were gone. Besides, if you generally accept the agnostic theory of knowledge, how can you convincingly carve out an exception to accommodate your belief in God?

b. Other liberals conceded that we have no *knowledge* of God, but argued that we are free to *believe* in God. Even Spencer would agree with that, for he would allow that we are free to believe whatever we like about the unknowable—provided we keep in mind that it is merely belief, not knowledge. Now, this sounds like traditional Christianity, which speaks all the time about "belief" (or its synonym "faith"). But for traditional Christianity belief was a kind of knowledge: it was a God-inspired conviction based on God's revelation. Not so with Spencerian belief. The kind of belief about the unknowable that Spencer would allow is a man-made guess, nothing more. The guess may be right or it may be wrong; but nobody can ever know because there is no way to compare the guess with the reality (the unknowable). But none of this discouraged many liberal Protestants from saying, "So what if we don't *know* about God? It is enough that we have *beliefs* about God."

c. Others argued that even if we are unable to know anything about God, nonetheless we can know about our personal religious experiences (our God experiences). If I have thoughts or feelings about God, if I have a sense that God is near me or that God is protecting me or that God is forgiving me my sins—if I have such thoughts or feelings or sensations, these things are happening, not in some supernatural realm, not in the realm of the unknowable, but *inside* me; they fall within the realm of the knowable. The great American philosopher-psychologist William James (1842–1910) devoted a very famous book to this topic, *The Varieties of Religious Experience*.[4] The trouble with this approach, however, is that while it certainly shows that the world is full of religious thoughts and feelings, and that these thoughts and feelings are tremendously important in the lives of many individuals, it doesn't show that the object of these thoughts and feelings—God—actually exists. Arguments along this line, agnostics could counter-argue, may prove that belief in God is useful or good, but they don't prove that belief in God is true. A pragmatist like James could reply that a belief is *true* to the degree that it is *useful*. But this pragmatist meaning of the word "true" is not the ordinary English meaning of the word.

d. Again, some liberals argued that Jesus, insofar as he was a human being, could be known by sense experience—that is, by the sense experience of those who saw him with their own eyes and listened to him with their own ears; and some of the results of this experience were written down in a number of ancient books (the four Gospels). In this limited but important way Jesus can be known by us today. And if, as traditional Christians have always believed, Jesus, in addition to being human, is also God, then in knowing Jesus we know God. However, to say this is to assume that we can know that Jesus was/is both man and God. And this assumption, agnosticism would say, is precisely what we have no right to make.

4. This was first published in 1902, based on James's Gifford Lectures of 1901–02. It has been published many times since then.

e. The most common response of liberal Christianity to agnosticism was to say that Christianity has little to do with knowledge (except of course for knowledge of the life and teachings of Jesus) and much to do with morality. Indeed, morality is the very essence of Christianity. Everything else is subordinate to morality. The function of all other elements of Christianity (doctrine and worship, for instance) is to preserve and promote good conduct. If we have no direct knowledge of God, so what? We have knowledge of the most important of all things, the difference between right and wrong. Further, we know how tremendously important moral goodness is: indeed, it is the most important thing in the world. Further still, if the great power behind the visible universe (that is, the unknowable power) has arranged the universe in such a way that moral goodness is the most important thing in the world, isn't this evidence that the unknowable is a God-like entity?

In any case, the agnostic theory of knowledge did not drive many Protestants into a disbelief of Christianity—except for those who, prior to having become acquainted with agnosticism, were already on the verge of unbelief. For those in the latter category, most of them young men, agnosticism was the final straw. It was the shove that pushed them over the cliff.

Darwinism

At first glance there would seem to be a flat and irreconcilable contradiction between the Darwinian theory of biological evolution and Protestant doctrine. For one thing, if the Darwinian theory is correct, the Bible's Genesis account of creation is incorrect; and this, as we saw in the previous chapter, for two reasons. First, because the Genesis account says that currently living species were created in their present form, whereas Darwin says the present forms emerged very gradually out of "lower" species. Second, because the Genesis account says creation took place in six days about six thousand years ago, whereas Darwin says that biological evolution has taken place over immense stretches of geological time.

Further, if the Genesis account of creation is in error, then the Bible is not inerrant or infallible. But the fundamental belief of Protestantism has always been that the Bible, the inspired word of God, *is* infallible. Let the Bible be in error, and the very foundation of Protestantism crumbles.

Prior to the emergence of Darwinism, the prevailing popular argument (at least in Britain and America) for the existence of God had been the "argument from Design" as formulated by William Paley (1743–1805) in his very influential book *Natural Theology* (1802). In a famous analogy Paley argued that if we were to find a complicated thing like a watch, it would never occur to us that the watch had just popped into existence or had developed automatically and spontaneously. We would conclude as soon as we examined the watch and its operation that it had been designed and made by an intelligent being. Likewise, when we examine a thing that is immensely more complicated than a watch, namely a living thing—a plant, an animal, a human being, even a small but complex part of a human such as the eye—we realize immediately that it too must be the creation of an intelligent mind; and when we look at the countless number of complex living things in the world, we realize that the world as a whole must be the creation of a vastly intelligent and immensely powerful mind. In short, it must be the creation of God.

But Darwinism seemed to destroy Paleyism. Random mutation plus natural selection plus inheritance plus immense stretches of time in which things might evolve gradually seemed to show that there is no need for a Supreme Mind as designer of living things. If Paley's Designer is no longer needed, the most popular argument for the existence of God is destroyed.

In response to the theory of evolution liberal Protestants became *theistic* evolutionists. They conceded that a process of Darwin-style evolution had indeed taken place, but they asserted that God has been the ultimate power behind this process. They agreed that Darwin was correct in his description of the process of evolution; he correctly explained *how* it took place. But he had said nothing about *why* it took place. He explained the process, but not the cause. For all that Darwin and his agnostic or atheistic supporters could know, God (or a Supreme Mind) may well lie behind evolution as its cause and ultimate explanation. We can accept random mutation and natural selection as the *apparent* cause of evolution, but we can still ask for a *real, ultimate* cause, and that may well be God.

But theistic evolutionists went further. It was not enough for them to say that God *may* be the ultimate cause of evolution. That was easy enough to say. For as long as there could be no proof that God was *not* the cause of evolution, it was obviously possible that God *could be* the cause. But the theistic evolutionists wanted to go much beyond saying that God *may be* the cause of biological evolution. They wanted to say that God *actually is* the ultimate cause. In making this case they were able to deploy a number of arguments.

1. According to Spencer and his fellow agnostics, we are free to hypothesize about the unknowable. Fine. But what is the most plausible hypothesis as to the ultimate cause of biological evolution? The same hypothesis as offered by Paley, the God-hypothesis. If a Supreme Intelligence was the most likely ultimate cause of the extraordinarily complex world that Paley thought himself to be living in, what was the most likely cause of the *even more complex* world that Darwin thought himself to be living in? Answer: an all-knowing and all-powerful Supreme Intelligence; in short, God. Perhaps we can no longer feel *certain*, as Paley felt certain, that the God-hypothesis is true; but it is by far the most *probable* hypothesis.

2. It had always been recognized by Christianity that God is a great mystery, a being who is incomprehensible. Spencer is telling Christians nothing new when he tells them that the ultimate foundation of reality is unknowable; he's just reminding them of what they have always believed. See, for example, John 1:18, "No one has ever seen God; the only Son, who is in the bosom of the Father, he has made him known." Or 1

John 4:12, "No man has ever seen God." Or Matthew 11:27, "All things have been delivered to me by my Father; and no one knows the Son except the Father, and no one knows the Father except the Son and any one to whom the Son chooses to reveal him." If the ultimate cause of evolution is mysterious, this is entirely compatible with the Christian belief as to the mysteriousness of God. If God is the ultimate cause of evolution, one would only expect that he would operate without showing his hand in an easily observable way.

3. Although in this life it is impossible for us to know God directly (Jesus is the only human who has ever known God directly), we can have some indirect knowledge of the Creator by careful observation of his creation—just as, in the presence of some great work of art (poetry, painting, sculpture, music, etc.), we gain, by studying the work of art, a glimpse of the mind of the artist even when he (or she) is totally anonymous. Think, for example, of the great Gothic cathedrals of the Middle Ages. We have no direct knowledge of the architects; usually we don't even know their names. But we have some "feel" for the minds of these great artists. Likewise we have some "feel" for the Great Architect who made the universe.

4. Finally, since God dwells in the realm of the unknowable, we cannot by searching find him. But God can find *us*, and can reveal himself to us. And so he has. He has revealed himself through the prophets and above all through Jesus Christ. The records of this divine revelation can be found in the Holy Bible.

What's more, Christian evolutionists took one step further in their acceptance of evolutionary theory. It's not just that faithful Christians can understand the theory of evolution as being compatible with the Bible; it's that evolution provides a clue for a better understanding of the Bible. If we keep the idea of evolution in mind when studying the Bible, we see that evolution—or gradual development—is God's normal way of working. We can see this in biological evolution; God creates the world gradually. We can see it in the development of the individual organism, e.g., a human being. Suzie Smith doesn't leap full-grown into the world, as Venus did from the forehead of Jove. No, Suzie begins as a teeny-weeny zygote and develops gradually into a fully developed human being. And we can see this gradualism in the development of God's revelation. He doesn't reveal his message all at once. No, he does it slowly over the course of many centuries. First comes Abraham; then Moses; then David and Solomon; then the prophets; then John the Baptist, the last of the prophets; and finally, the culmination and fulfillment of this long and gradual revelation, Jesus Christ. Evolution, to repeat, is God's normal way of working.

The Higher Criticism

The "higher" critics of the Bible had during the nineteenth century done a lot of damage to the traditional Protestant idea of both the Old and the New Testaments. Not all the higher critics agreed on everything. Some were more extreme in their skeptical criticism, some more moderate. Some were frankly anti-Christian, some were believing and practicing Protestants. But taken collectively they did a lot of damage to the basic Protestant ideas that the Bible is the revealed word of God and that the Bible is infallible.

How did liberal Protestants get around this difficulty? How did they acknowledge that there was much truth to be found in the higher criticism while at the same time holding on to their traditional notion that the Bible is the foundation of the Protestant religion?

Two strategic moves were essential to their carrying out this at-first-glance-impossible task. First, instead of saying that the Bible is God's revelation, liberals said that the Bible is the *record* of God's revelation. This revelation has taken place gradually, on a step-by-step basis, over thousands of years. At first we humans, or rather the Hebrews of old, had a crude idea of God and his dealings with human beings. This crude understanding is exhibited in the older parts of the Old Testament, where God is often represented in less-than-perfect anthropomorphic terms; he is a powerful king who insists on obedience, and he gets angry when his will is defied; very like the human kings of the ancient Mideast.

With time, however, the idea of God gets morally refined, grows less and less anthropomorphic; or if it remains anthropomorphic, the *anthropos* in question is a man of much higher moral and intellectual capacity. By the time of the New Testament the idea of God—the idea as it presented itself to the mind of Jesus—is a very lofty idea indeed: the idea of a perfect God than whom none can be better. It is now the idea of God as a loving father, a father of mercy who is willing to sacrifice the life of his son, which is also his own life, for the good of his children.

The second move was this. God's revelation takes place at the moment humans receive this revelation; which is to say, at the moment when humans—or at least one human, who then communicates his discovery to others—come to realize something new and better about God. God's revelations are the same thing as man's discoveries about God; they are two sides of the same coin. To date, the most perfect of these revelations/discoveries is the one revealed to, or discovered by, Jesus of Nazareth, that Jewish religious genius from the age of Augustus and Tiberius—namely, the stupendous insight by Jesus that God is a loving and merciful father.

If you define revelation in these terms, you can say of the Bible, even after the higher critics have done their worst, that it is "the word of God" because it is a great anthology of books that record God's progressive revelation to man; or (what comes to the same thing) it records man's progressive discovery of the nature of God. The Bible, then, can continue to be the solid basis of Protestantism even though the Bible is no longer considered infallible; even though, indeed, it is acknowledged to be far from infallible. Unlike premodern Protestants, who imagined that every word of the Bible counted as a revelation from God, the liberal or modernist Protestant can freely admit that the Bible abounds in errors—errors as to authorship, errors as to historical facts, errors as to the record of words spoken, even some of the words attributed to Jesus. But among all these errors can be found amazing discoveries/revelations about God and his nature—like nuggets of gold found in a muddy stream. The writers of the books of the

Bible may not themselves have been inspired, but they have given us a record of inspired discoveries.

☙ ❧

The more that liberal Protestants de-emphasized the doctrinal content of Christianity, the more they emphasized the ethical content—the more, in other words, they held that morality is the essence of Christianity. Remember Matthew Arnold's definition of religion as "morality touched with emotion." But the morality in question wasn't always the traditional Christian morality. Often it was a new morality. Not a new morality that discarded any portion of the old morality.[5] No, but a new morality that *added to* the old morality.

The liberal Protestant response to the agnostic attack on Christianity largely coincided in time with the emergence of "the social question"—that is, the question of the place of the laboring classes in modern society. How were wage workers to be treated in the rapidly expanding urban-industrial-capitalist society? Did they and their families have rights that it was the duty of government to protect? Or were they to be left to do the best they could in a *laissez-faire* regime of unregulated capitalism? The "social Darwinists"[6] favored the latter answer. A variety of voices called for the former answer—including socialists, labor unions, progressive politicians, even the pope,[7] and liberal Protestants.

The liberal Protestant response to the social question was named "the Social Gospel." There were many representatives of the Social Gospel movement, but none more enduringly famous than Walter Rauschenbusch (1861–1918). He had been working in the Social Gospel field for two decades, first as a liberal Baptist

---

5. Discarding portions of traditional Protestant morality didn't happen until the late twentieth century when liberal Protestantism gave its endorsement to the sexual revolution.

6. They should have been called "social Spencerians," for it was Herbert Spencer who favored unregulated capitalism, not Charles Darwin, who had nothing to say on the question.

7. Pope Leo XIII in his famous encyclical of 1891, *On the Condition of the Working Classes*, commonly known as *Rerum Novarum*.

minister and later as a seminary professor, before he published in 1907 his best-known book, *Christianity and the Social Crisis*, a superb summary of Social Gospel ideas.

According to the Social Gospellers, Christianity has, at least in principle, the answers to the social question. Old-fashioned Protestantism told us how to live our private individual lives: don't lie, don't cheat, don't steal, don't get drunk, don't fornicate, don't commit adultery, and be kind to your family, your friends, your immediate neighbors, etc. It assumed that if we do these things, if we obey the commandments in our personal lives, the wellbeing of society will take care of itself. Social Gospel liberals disagreed. They held that society, acting through both government and nongovernment agencies, must take positive steps to regulate the economy and provide for the wellbeing of the working classes. What steps? Steps inspired by Christian love. Steps that Jesus would recommend were he among us today.

Thanks to the Social Gospel, liberal Protestantism had a broader notion of morality than that held by old-fashioned Protestants. To be a good Christian, it was not enough to obey the commandments. One also had to promote "social justice." That is, one had to work for institutional reforms that would improve the hitherto miserable conditions in which the working classes often had to work and live. In practice this meant that one had to support labor unions, workers' compensation laws, trust-busting, and government regulation of big industry. The early years of the twentieth century constituted what historians call "the Progressive Era," and the Social Gospellers generally supported the social reform agenda of secular progressives.

Allow me make a few closing observations.

First, I have just used the expression "social justice." It is an expression much used today, in the early twenty-first century, by both religious liberals and secular liberals. Today many religious liberals consider that a strong commitment to social justice more than makes up for a laxity in sexual morals. Take for example

Martin Luther King. For his heroic, life-sacrificing work in the field of racial justice, religious liberals would generally consider him to be nothing less than a saint, even though we now know what only a few knew during his lifetime: that MLK was often guilty of adultery.

Second, it was during this Protestant era—the response-to-agnosticism era—that religious liberals first began taking their moral cues from secular moralists. Hitherto the moral leaders in America had been Protestant ministers, aided and abetted by fervent Protestant laypersons (e.g., Harriet Beecher Stowe). By early in the twentieth century Protestant moralists—even though they no longer had a monopoly on giving moral instruction, for secular moralists were making their voices heard as never before—still played a major role; and they continued to play this role until well into the twentieth century.[8] However, nowadays (early twenty-first century) liberal Protestant moralists do little more than tag along behind secular progressive moralists. If, for example, secular progressives give their endorsement to abortion rights, to homosexuality, to same-sex marriage, to transgender rights, liberal Protestant moralists say in effect, "We second that motion." Liberal Protestant moralists no longer have any moral ideas of their own; all their new ideas are borrowed from secular progressive moralists.

Finally, while throughout this book my sympathies as an author mainly lie with Protestant traditionalists, not Protestant liberals, I confess that I sometimes have strong sympathies with the liberals. Earlier I expressed sympathy with Ralph Waldo Emerson. I also sympathize with the Social Gospellers. If today we live in an America in which capitalism is not "unbridled," in which labor unions are free to operate, in which the public is protected from unsafe food and drugs, in which almost everybody receives (or will receive) an old-age pension (Social Security), in which occupational safety laws are operative, in which higher education is open to all, in which race discrimination is prohibited by law,

8. I remember that when I was a boy in the 1940s and 1950s, growing up Catholic in a predominantly Catholic industrial city (Pawtucket, Rhode Island), the local newspaper still treated a certain local Congregational minister—not any Catholic priest and not any secular moralist—as the city's semi-official moral authority.

in which environmental protection laws are in place—all this is due, not entirely but in no small measure, to the impetus to social reform given by Social Gospellers more than a century ago. I for one am grateful.

10

Lyman Abbott

A SPLENDID EXAMPLE OF the liberal Protestant response to the agnostic attack on Christianity was given by Lyman Abbott (1835–1922), the successor to Henry Ward Beecher in the pulpit of the Plymouth Congregational Church in Brooklyn. Beecher, the son of the Calvinist theologian Lyman Beecher and the brother of Harriet Beecher Stowe (author of *Uncle Tom's Cabin*), was perhaps the best-known American Protestant preacher and minister in the second half of the nineteenth century and certainly the best-known *liberal* preacher and minister. When the three-part agnostic attack on Christianity arrived, Beecher made characteristically liberal accommodations.

After his death, Beecher's ample mantle fell on the shoulders of Abbott, a prolific author who wrote, among many other things, a biography of Beecher.

One of Abbott's books was titled *The Theology of an Evolutionist*. In this book he responded to the three agnostic attacks on Christianity. He responded (1) to the Darwinian attack by accepting—nay, by warmly embracing—the theory of evolution; (2) to the higher criticism attack by accepting many of the skeptical results of the higher critics; and (3) to the agnostic theory of knowledge attack by denying that our limited capacity for knowledge makes us incapable of having knowledge of God. He argued that the world, both the world of nature and the world of human history, is a manifestation of God; and so we can get to know God by studying the world.

Abbott made the typical liberal distinction between religion and theology. "Religion," Abbott said, "is the life of God in the soul of man."[1] Theology is not religion; it is a *theory* about religion. While theology changes from age to age, religion remains the same. The religion of Christianity is what it always was, but the theology of Christianity, which has changed many times over the centuries, is due for another change. Abbott's distinction between religion and theology is the distinction made decades earlier by that great liberal, that Unitarian-transcendentalist, Theodore Parker, in his essay on the permanent and transient in Christianity. The old theology, according to Abbott, was now out of date; it is time for a new theology, an evolutionary theology. That's what Abbott was offering.

He warmly embraced the theory of evolution, not just biological evolution but a far more general kind of evolution. He made a crucial distinction between Darwinism and evolution. He agreed that the Darwinian theory of biological evolution (struggle for existence, natural selection, survival of the fittest, etc.) was a good *description* of the history of living things on the planet Earth. It described the *how* of that history, but it said nothing about the *why*. God is the *why*. Besides, the process of evolution was a much broader thing than biological evolution. Biological evolution was a striking example of evolution, but there were many other examples. For what is evolution? It is "God's way of doing things," said Abbott, borrowing these words from the philosopher John Fiske.[2] That is to say, God's way may be described as "the way of growth, or development, or evolution, terms which are substantially

---

1. Abbott, *Theology of an Evolutionist*, 1.
2. Abbott, *Theology of an Evolutionist*, 3.

synonymous."[3] "The creed of the evolutionist is all embodied in the statement that life is growth."[4]

In the old theology, God was *above* the world and he *made* the world. Abbott's God is an immanent God, a God present in the world. Nor does Abbott's God *make* the world; rather the world is a *manifestation* of God. Perhaps we can say (though Abbott doesn't use precisely this analogy) that the world of nature manifests God the way heat and light manifest the sun. The sun doesn't deliberately and intentionally manufacture heat and light; no, heat and light are spontaneous manifestations of the sun's nature. The laws of nature are the laws of God's being. This sounds like pantheism, yet Abbott quite explicitly denies that he is a pantheist. God may be *in* nature, but he is also *above* nature; he is both immanent and transcendent. "As the artist transcends all his pictures . . . so God transcends all manifestations of God."[5]

Herbert Spencer had said that the reality underlying all the world's appearances is "an Infinite and Eternal Energy from which all things proceed."[6] Abbot adopts this as his definition of God—except that while Spencer holds that this power is unknown and unknowable, Abbott holds that this power is at least to some degree knowable. And further, it is personal. It has knowledge and will; it has plans for the world, and is steadily but surely bringing these plans to fruition. This movement toward fruition is what Christians mean, or at least should mean, by "evolution."

God has manifested himself by degrees. We may say of all things in nature what the Bible says of Adam and Eve, that they are made in the "image and likeness" of God. But some things are better and higher images than others. First God shows himself in the world of inanimate nature. Then he shows himself in the world of plants, the world of animate but non-sensate beings. Then he shows himself in the world of animals and other living things that have powers of sensation and locomotion. Next he shows

---

3. Abbott, *Theology of an Evolutionist*, 9.

4. Abbott, *Theology of an Evolutionist*, vi.

5. Abbott, *Theology of an Evolutionist*, 71.

6. Abbott, *Theology of an Evolutionist*, 13.

himself in the world of human beings, animals with intellect and will—with a capacity, that is, for rational knowledge and moral goodness (or badness). Best of all, he manifests himself in Jesus Christ, the best of all humans and the highest image of God. "Jesus Christ," Abbott says, "is the supreme product of evolution in human history."[7] This is what we mean, or should mean, when we say that Jesus was God Incarnate.

Was Jesus different in kind from ordinary human beings? Or was he different only in degree? "The divinity in man," Abbott answers, "is not different in kind from the divinity in Christ, because it is not different in kind from the divinity in God."[8] Jesus Christ, magnificent though he was, is not the end and summit of the evolutionary process; he is not God's ultimate manifestation.

> And the consummation of evolution . . . the consummation of this long process of divine manifestation . . . will not be until the whole human race becomes what Christ was, until the incarnation so spreads out from the one man of Nazareth that it fills the whole human race, and all humanity becomes an incarnation of the divine, the infinite and all-loving Spirit. What Jesus was, humanity is becoming.[9]

As for the Bible, the Christian evolutionist "is not in the least troubled by finding errors in it; he expects to find such errors."[10] After all, if we understand the Bible as the product of religious evolution, we won't expect it to be inerrant or infallible.[11]

> The Bible is a record of man's laboratory work in the spiritual realm, a history of the dawning of the consciousness of God and of the divine life in the soul of man. It contains the story of his spiritual aspirations, his dim, half-seen visions of truth, his fragments of knowledge,

---

7. Abbott, *Theology of an Evolutionist*, 74.

8. Abbott, *Theology of an Evolutionist*, 73.

9. Abbott, *Theology of an Evolutionist*, 75–76.

10. Abbott, *Theology of an Evolutionist*, 56.

11. Abbott, *Theology of an Evolutionist*, 60.

his blunders, his struggles with the errors of others, and with his own prejudices.[12]

The Bible shows us that God's revelations—or (what comes to the same thing) man's discoveries about God—are not an all-at-once kind of thing. Instead they arrive gradually, often mixed with error; just as we might expect if we realize that God's way of working is to proceed by way of evolution.

In the course of his book Abbott affirms his belief in the resurrection of Jesus, which he contends is "the best-attested fact of ancient history."[13] He affirms his belief in many, but not all, Biblical miracles (See his chapters IX and X). Whenever Abbott affirms his belief in a traditional Christian doctrine, he does so by showing that this doctrine is consistent with evolutionary theory. For instance, he affirms his belief in life after death, and in doing so asks the rhetorical question: Why would God, having spent billions of years in making a world that leads up to the emergence of human beings, allow these ultimate products of evolution to perish? He quotes the philosopher John Fiske: "God is not like a child that builds a house of cards to blow it down again."[14] Without immortality, Abbott says, "all evolution would be meaningless."[15]

Abbott does not affirm his belief in either the virgin birth or the Trinity. He plainly rejects the theory of a substitutionary atonement. Jesus suffered and died, he says, to free us from sin, not from the *penalty* due to sin.[16]

If we start as Christians, Abbott argues, we find that the theory of evolution gives a very plausible explanation of our religion. Or if we start as evolutionists, we find that Christianity is just the religion that we might expect from an Infinite and Eternal Energy.

12. Abbott, *Theology of an Evolutionist*, 58.

13. Abbott, *Theology of an Evolutionist*, 129.

14. Abbott, *Theology of an Evolutionist*, 171.

15. Abbott, *Theology of an Evolutionist*, 173.

16. Abbott, *Theology of an Evolutionist*, 110.

11

Fundamentalism versus Modernism

THE FIRST DIVISION OF American Protestantism into liberal and conservative camps came, as we have seen, at the beginning of the nineteenth century with the emergence in New England of Unitarianism and Universalism. The former deviated from the Protestant Consensus by its rejection of the Trinity and the divinity of Christ; the latter deviated by its rejection of hell or eternal damnation. Despite their differences from one another (among which was that Unitarianism was an urban phenomenon, Universalism rural), both, we may say, were motivated by the same "spirit," the spirit of modernizing Christianity, the spirit of aligning Christianity with currently fashionable secular beliefs and values. It was fitting therefore that eventually the two denominations merged into a single denomination, the Unitarian Universalist Association (UUA), even though the merger didn't happen until 1961. (One wonders what took them so long.)

But Unitarianism and Universalism were numerically small things in comparison with mainstream American Protestantism, which was a large thing, a very large thing indeed, stretching in the early years of the USA from New England to Georgia and from the Atlantic coast to the Mississippi River, and by the middle

1850s stretching from Maine to Florida and from the Atlantic to the Pacific. With the Unitarian and Universalist exceptions, the Protestant Consensus still held throughout the world of American Protestantism until the years soon after the Civil War.

The truly substantial division between conservative (traditional) and liberal (modernist) Protestantism didn't arrive until the agnostic attack on Christianity in the last third of the nineteenth century. More precisely, it didn't arrive until liberal/modernists began responding to that agnostic attack.[1] Traditionalists detected in that modernist response an accommodation to the forces of anti-Christianity, above all with regard to the authority of the Bible. Modernists accepted the theory of biological evolution, provided this was understood to be *theistic* evolution; but even so, this was tantamount to rejecting a literal reading of the Genesis account of creation. Further, modernists accepted many of the results of the higher criticism of the Bible. As traditionalists saw things, modernists tried to deceive unlearned Christians by continuing to speak of the Bible as the "word of God," but they didn't really mean this. They meant that it was a "record" of God's revelations even though much of the Bible was unhistorical, mythological, erroneous, etc. In effect, modernists were undermining, if not totally rejecting, the authority of the Bible. But the Bible, the whole Bible, and nothing but the Bible had from the early 1500s been the one and only religious authority of Protestantism. Reject the Bible, and you reject Protestantism itself; and reject Protestantism, the true version of Christianity, and you reject Christianity itself. You reject the religion of Jesus Christ, the true religion of God. That, from the conservative point of view, is what the modernists were up to. Whatever the piety and good intentions of many modernists (generally speaking, they were very pious and very well-intentioned), modernism was similar to the agnostic movement in that they

1. From this point on in the book I will feel free to use the words "liberal" and "modernist" interchangeably, since it was not until after the Civil War that it became quite clear that liberal Protestantism is, in its essence, little more than an attempt to accommodate Christianity to modern secular beliefs and values; and as these modern beliefs and values change with the passing decades, so does the content of liberal Protestantism.

both (in the judgment of traditional Protestants) tended to the destruction of Christianity. The difference between the two was that the agnostics aimed quite knowingly and quite openly at this destruction, while liberal or modernist Protestants, although they didn't truly *aim* at it, were bringing it about gradually and deceitfully—and perhaps even more effectively than agnostics.

∽ ∾

Conservative Protestantism reacted to this betrayal (as they saw it) of Protestantism by doubling down, and more than doubling down, on old-fashioned Protestantism. Great numbers of conservative Protestants became fundamentalists, and conservative Protestantism became, at least to a very great extent, *fundamentalism.* This name came from a series of books titled *The Fundamentals.*[2] The series contained nearly one hundred articles written by conservative ministers, theologians, Bible scholars, college presidents, etc. These authors came from England, Scotland, Ireland, Canada, the USA, and in one case from Germany; included among them were some of the most notable names in the world of Protestant theology, e.g., Benjamin Warfield, Bishop Ryle, C. I. Scofield. These articles covered a very wide variety of topics, among which were the following:

- a defense of a literal reading of the Bible, including Genesis.

- a defense of a number of specific Christian doctrines, e.g., the virgin birth, the divinity of Christ, the resurrection.

- attacks on Darwinism and the higher criticism.

- attacks on what were seen as seriously defective versions of Christianity, e.g., Roman Catholicism, Mormonism, Jehovah's Witnesses, Christian Science.

- an attack on socialism.

---

2. These were originally published in twelve volumes, beginning in 1909. In 1917 they were republished in four volumes, and these four volumes were again republished in 1998 by Baker Books.

And much more—the underlying message throughout being that traditional Protestantism is the one and only true version of Christianity. In effect, *The Fundamentals* was a lengthy and learned version of the message contained in the song, "Gimme That Old-Time Religion."[3]

For decades, from the 1880s forward, the fight between fundamentalists and modernists went on, growing ever more intense, often splitting denominations into two warring factions. More and more, liberals seemed to gain the upper hand in this fight, for they were winning to their side Protestants who were better educated and more urbanized, just at a moment in American history when levels of education and urbanization were rising rapidly. Many features of fundamentalism made it unattractive to well-educated Protestants, but the feature that made it *most* unattractive was its rejection of the theory of biological evolution. For to agree with this rejection was in effect to reject a number of well-established modern sciences: biology, paleontology, geology, and physical astronomy. It was not easy to persuade well-educated people to make these rejections; hence they drifted in the direction of liberal Protestantism, whose ranks rapidly expanded.

The battle between the two sides, though it began in the 1880s, came to a head in the 1920s, and is illustrated in the careers of two men: on the liberal side, Harry Emerson Fosdick (1878–1969); on the fundamentalist side, William Jennings Bryan (1860–1925).

Bryan was a politician and a great public speaker. His magnificent "Cross of Gold" speech at the 1896 Democratic National Convention inspired the convention to make him the Democratic nominee for President of the United States, to this day the youngest

3. According to a Wikipedia article on the subject, this hymn dates from 1873—which is early in the era of the agnostic attack on Christianity and the liberal Protestant response to that attack (Wikipedia, "Old-Time Religion"). The song is a sign, it seems to me, that rank-and-file traditional Protestants were already aware that their religion was under attack by those who would modernize Christianity.

person either major party has ever nominated. He was defeated by William McKinley in 1896, again by McKinley in 1900, and by William Howard Taft in 1908. He was Woodrow Wilson's Secretary of State for two years (1913–15).

Bryan was a Presbyterian, a fundamentalist who held that the Bible is the literal word of God and that the theory of evolution is false and dangerous.[4] (It should be noted, however, that he held that the six days of creations were not necessarily twenty-four-hour days. Instead the word "day" in Genesis may signify an immensely long era of time.) His objection to the Darwinian theory was twofold. First, it was un-Biblical and therefore false. Second, it could be used, and indeed *was* being used, to justify a morality according to which strong nations have the right to take advantage of weaker nations and strong individuals have the right to take advantage of weaker individuals. For the strong could argue, borrowing the biological vocabulary of Darwin and applying it to socio-economic situations, that human progress is the result of a "struggle for existence" in which only the "fit" survive, and only the fit *should* survive. At all events, as he drifted away from politics in the late 1910s, Bryan moved more and more into using his great oratorical skills to lead the fundamentalist fight against agnosticism and liberal Protestantism, and especially against their mutual embrace of the theory of evolution. He supported the idea that states should forbid the teaching of evolution in the public schools. A number of states did precisely that. Among these was Tennessee, and in 1925 a teacher in Dayton, Tennessee, John Scopes, deliberately violated that ban in order to provoke a test case in hopes that the court would declare this ban on teaching evolution to be unconstitutional.

This was the famous "monkey trial."[5] The lawyer for defendant Scopes was Clarence Darrow, a famous agnostic who was

4. A detailed statement of Bryan's views is given in his book *In His Image*.

5. For a popular account of the trial, see the movie *Inherit the Wind* (1960), starring Frederic March, Spencer Tracy, and Gene Kelly, the movie being closely based on a Broadway play of a few years earlier. Unfortunately, the movie and the play give an unfair caricature of Bryan. For a more ample and more correct view of what happened at Dayton, see a book that won the Pulitzer Prize for history, *A Summer for the Gods* (1998), by Edward Larson.

America's leading criminal defense attorney. Bryan, a lawyer by profession, volunteered to assist the prosecution. The trial, it seemed, was to be a clash of titans, Darrow versus Bryan. Journalists from all over the country flocked to Dayton to cover the trial, which was taking place at the height of the long-running struggle between fundamentalists and modernists. It promised to be a climactic moment in that struggle—and it delivered on that promise; it turned out to be precisely that, a climactic moment. The trial was even covered by that new medium, radio. Quite understandably, the trial was treated by the press as a matter of great national importance, and it was closely followed by much of the public.

Darrow's strategy involved putting scientists on the stand who would testify that the Darwinian theory is sound science and therefore deserves to be taught in the schools. But the judge wouldn't allow this. The point of the trial, he said, was not to determine whether Darwinism is true or not; the point was to determine if young Mr. Scopes had broken a Tennessee law. Frustrated in this attempt, Darrow surprisingly invited Bryan to take the stand as an expert witness on the Bible, and Bryan, foolishly as it turned out, accepted the invitation. Now Bryan had a great knowledge of the Bible, but he was neither a minister nor a theologian. And while he had a very good layman's knowledge of the theory of evolution, he wasn't a trained scientist either. And while he was a lawyer by profession, he had rarely or never practiced law for decades. The upshot of it all was that Darrow made Bryan look foolish on the stand as the latter made fumbling and bumbling attempts to reconcile scientific facts with the Biblical account of creation.

The court's verdict went against Scopes, who was fined one hundred dollars. But in the far more important court—the "court of public opinion"—Scopes won, Darrow won, the evolutionists won, and so therefore did liberal Protestantism win. For the public had followed the trial, at least much of the educated public had followed it, and had come away with the strong impression that the anti-evolutionists were fools; from which it seemed to follow that fundamentalism was foolish. If so, only liberal Protestantism made sense.

As for poor Bryan—a few days later, still in Dayton, he died of a stroke.

Harry Emerson Fosdick (1878–1969) was probably the best-known liberal Protestant minister of the first half of the twentieth century. He wasn't *awfully* liberal; in comparison to liberal Protestants of the early twenty-first century, he appears to have been almost conservative. For he rejected only small portions of the Protestant Consensus, e.g., the virgin birth of Jesus. But he rejected the crucial thing, the infallibility of the Bible. Once a Protestant rejects that, he has opened the door to many other rejections. Fosdick himself did not make many of these possible rejections, but he paved the way for later and more thoroughgoing liberal/modernist Protestants.

Fosdick was born in Buffalo, educated at Colgate College and the Union Theological Seminary (where he later taught), and ordained as a Baptist minister in 1903. Despite being a Baptist, he was called in 1918 to be pastor of New York City's First Presbyterian Church, where in 1922 he delivered his famous sermon in defense of modernist Protestantism, "Shall the Fundamentalists Win?" Fosdick was already rather well-known nationally as the author of a number of religious books, but this sermon multiplied his fame (or notoriety, if you prefer) many times over, making him a great hero among modernists, a great villain among fundamentalists. This sermon provoked a tremendous controversy among Presbyterians, some of whom wished to censure him, while others (including John Foster Dulles, who in the 1950s would be Eisenhower's Secretary of State) rushed to his defense. Leaving the Presbyterians in 1924, Fosdick became the pastor of the Park Avenue Baptist Church, whose most famous member was the philanthropist John D. Rockefeller Jr., son and heir of the founder of Standard Oil. The younger Rockefeller, a great fan and supporter of Fosdick, built the magnificent Riverside Church in Manhattan, a nondenominational (or inter-denominational) Christian church with Fosdick as its first pastor, serving until his retirement in 1946.

Among other social causes, Fosdick was a notable champion of racial justice.

For decades Fosdick was the nation's best-known and most influential liberal Protestant minister. His opinions reached a vast audience, not only at Riverside Church and other speaking venues, but even more in his weekly radio broadcasts and in his many books, more than three dozen. His liberalism, as noted above, was rather a tame thing compared with that of twenty-first century liberal Protestantism, but it can be argued that no American liberal Protestant was ever more important, for it was he, more than any other man, who persuaded millions of American Protestants that it is permissible to modify the faith in order to keep up with the times.

In the aftermath of the "monkey trial" it seemed to many Protestants, probably most of them, that the great struggle between modernism and fundamentalism was essentially over. Modernism had won. Fundamentalism, though it would no doubt survive for a while in some of America's rural, small-town, and backwoods regions, had been defeated and would fade away in time. For persons who had studied history, literature, and science in high school, and even more so for persons who had studied these subjects in college, a fundamentalist version of Christianity was becoming quite impossible. If Protestantism is to survive in the USA—and it *must* survive, for without Protestant Christianity what will become of the USA?—it will have to be a modernist Protestant version of Christianity.

During the 1930s (the years of the Great Depression), the 1940s (the years of World War II and the early Cold War), and even into the 1950s, the triumph of modernistic Protestantism seemed to most people to be complete. When educated people, whether Protestant or Catholic or Jewish or secularist, thought of Protestantism in America, they thought of modernistic Protestantism. They were aware of Protestant fundamentalism, but they thought of it as being a fossilized relic of a more primitive America.

Catholicism was the religion of a still-alien minority. And Judaism was so numerically small that it hardly mattered. The more or less official religion of the United States was Protestantism, as modernized by Harry Emerson Fosdick and his like-minded fellow liberals.

But in the late 1940s and early 1950s there was on the cultural horizon a fundamentalist cloud, no bigger than a man's hand at first, but growing. The name of this cloud was Billy Graham, and the Protestant Christianity he preached was no longer called (except by its enemies) fundamentalism; for "fundamentalist" had by this time become something of a dirty word. Instead the religion of Billy Graham was now called "evangelical Christianity." But its provenance was fundamentalism; in essence it was the same thing except that it had a "softer" tone. The "old-time religion" was making a comeback. And not just in America's backwoods. Graham, a brilliant preacher and magnetic personality, was holding multi-day revivals in such big cities as New York and Los Angeles; even in London, England. To the astonishment of many intelligent persons who had predicted the future of American Protestantism, Graham and his followers subscribed to the Protestant Consensus—the Consensus that had been formulated by the sixteenth-century Reformers.

By the 1960s and 1970s and 1980s sociologists began noting that modernistic Protestantism was in significant numerical decline. The mainline Protestant denominations dominated by liberal seminary professors and liberal ministers were not growing in step with the growth of the American population; worse still, they were shrinking in absolute numbers. I mean such denominations as The Episcopal Church, the Presbyterian Church USA, the United Methodist Church, the Evangelical Lutheran Church of America, the American Baptist Church, and the United Church of Christ. Not only did they shrink in numbers, but they shrank in social influence. No longer was liberal Protestantism the unofficial religion of America.

By the 1960s—the decade when young people rebelled against racism, the Vietnam War, and authority in general, and rallied in favor of sex, drugs, and new kinds of music—secular humanism was on the rise. Many people, especially young people, were turning against Christianity either in theory or in practice or both. The form of Christianity they were turning against was modernistic Protestantism, for the modernism of Harry Emerson Fosdick and his theological peers was no longer modern enough for the rebels of the 1960s. By the 1970s American Catholicism too was in decline.[6]

Why has support for modernist Protestantism declined and support for evangelical Protestantism risen in the last sixty years or so? I suggest the following explanation. During this time Protestant modernism has more and more come to resemble secular humanism in its beliefs and values. However, if you hold secular humanist beliefs and values, you don't need to attend or belong to a church to have these beliefs and values validated and reinforced. You can get them reinforced by reading the *New York Times* and other major secular publications; by consuming the products put out by the entertainment industry (e.g., TV, movies, popular music); by getting your TV news from MSNBC or CNN; and by attending secular colleges and universities. On the other hand, if you hold traditional Christian beliefs and values, you won't get these reinforced anywhere except in traditional Christian institutions, above all in evangelical churches and schools.

6. See my book, *The Decline and Fall of Catholicism in America.*

12

The Third Assault

The Sexual Revolution

As we have seen earlier in the book, first came the deistic attack on Christianity, and then the liberal Protestant accommodation to that attack, Unitarianism. Next came the agnostic attack on Christianity, and then the liberal Protestant accommodation to that attack, modernism. Finally came the sexual revolution attack on Christianity, and then the liberal Protestant accommodation to that attack.

In this chapter we'll look at the sexual revolution. In the next chapter we'll look at the liberal Protestant response to the sexual revolution. And in the chapter after that we'll look at the Evangelical response both to the sexual revolution itself and to the liberal Protestant accommodation to that revolution.

When I speak of the sexual revolution, what I have in mind is the great and sudden change in sexual morality that took place in the United States beginning in the early 1960s. If we want a convenient date to mark the beginning of the revolution, we may say 1960, the year in which the birth control pill was approved by the US Food and Drug Administration. I don't mean that it was "the pill" which all by itself caused the revolution, although it made a considerable contribution to it. But its appearance was an important symbolic moment.

When I speak of the "great and sudden change in sexual morality" I don't have in mind a change in sexual *behavior* only; even more I have in mind a change in the *moral evaluations* of sexual behavior. Behavior did change, certainly. Almost overnight, it seemed, conduct that had been morally condemned from time out of mind—such conduct as sexual intercourse between unmarried young persons, sexual cohabitation between unmarried persons, out-of-wedlock pregnancies, and abortion—became widespread; and not just widespread in practice, but widely approved of. What had been almost universally considered to be wrong (even by those who engaged in such practices) was now widely considered to be right, and among the younger generation almost *universally* considered to be right. Further, it was right in two senses of the word "right." That is, it was considered to be right in the sense of *permissible*, and also right in the sense of *obligatory*. When Mary Sue went to college she didn't just have a *right* to go to bed with her boyfriend; she had something like a *duty* to do so, a duty to herself, to all of womankind, and to society at large. If she graduated with her virginity intact she was suffering from some kind of shameful infirmity.

Although this revolution seemed to be a sudden explosion, there had been a long and gradual buildup to it though most of the twentieth century, especially since the end of World War I. Some of the highpoints of this buildup were the following.

1. Feminism. The movement for women's equality had begun in the nineteenth century and grew greatly in strength early in the twentieth. Among other things, this demand for equality called into question, at least by implication, the traditional "double standard" that had imposed a much stricter code of sexual morality on women than on men. If society was relatively tolerant

of, say, premarital sex among men, shouldn't it be equally tolerant of premarital sex among women?

2. Hollywood. Not only did movies often deal with narratives that were more or less erotic in character, but it was generally understood by movie fans that the private lives of many movie stars were, to say the least, sexually liberated. Hollywood was imagined to be a kind of sexual paradise.

3. Margaret Sanger and the birth control movement. Both Protestants and Catholics had traditionally considered contraception, including marital contraception, to be immoral. In the years between the two World Wars Protestant resistance to marital contraception largely collapsed, and resistance among lay Catholics was weakened.

4. Bertrand Russell. One of the world's most famous philosophers defended fornication, unmarried cohabitation, and (in some situations) adultery. See his popular book *Marriage and Morals*.

5. Sigmund Freud. While Freud called for a certain relaxation of sexual standards, many of his American fans thought, quite erroneously, that he had called for extensive sexual freedom. On the contrary, Freud thought that a considerable amount of sexual repression was needed for civilization to thrive.[1] But he thought that this repression was often overdone, especially with regard to middle-class women, and should therefore be relaxed. Many of his American fans who either didn't read him carefully or didn't read him at all got the mistaken idea that Freud believed that the more sexual freedom, the better.

6. Margaret Mead. In the 1920s a young American anthropologist, Margaret Mead (1901–78), spent some months in Samoa interviewing unmarried young women about their sex lives. This led to Mead's famous and influential book, *Coming of Age in Samoa* (1928), in which she reported that Samoan boys and girls were free to have numerous premarital sex

---

1. See Freud's book *Civilization and Its Discontents*.

relationships, and that this freedom appeared to have little or nothing in the way of harmful consequences. Most notably, Samoan teens had none of the psychological "storm and stress" typical of American teens. This book was required reading for millions of American college students in the two decades following World War II.

7. The Kinsey Reports. Although these two reports (one on men in 1948, the other on women in 1952) were of questionable scientific merit, they concluded that Americans, both married and unmarried, were far less chaste than had been generally supposed, and that homosexuality was more common than had been generally supposed. Not many people actually read the reports, which were lengthy and laden with boring statistics. But due to extensive reporting in newspapers and magazines, tens of millions knew second- and thirdhand of the reports and their more sensational contents. Many Americans concluded that a certain degree of sexual immorality was more or less "normal," and if normal, then not truly immoral.

8. The birth control pill. Women could now have sex with small risk and little inconvenience. Men and women were now, for the first time in human history, equal partners with regard to nonmarital sex. The "pill" had been invented so that married couples could intelligently "space" their children. But it was inevitable that it would also be used by unmarried couples to facilitate risk-free sex.

In any case the stage had been set, the pump had been primed; and by the time a pampered generation that had grown up in post-World War II prosperity came of age, the sexual revolution was virtually inevitable.

❧ ❧

This revolution in sexual morality was in effect, if only rarely in intention, an anti-Christianity phenomenon. Some of the young revolutionaries understood this. Many others, both Protestants and Catholics, did not; they had the idea that they could retain the religion of their childhood while at the same time profiting (as they saw it) from the new ethic of sexual freedom. They were mistaken in this idea. For Christianity had from its beginning been a religion that demanded a high degree of sexual restraint from its adherents. And this sexual restraint was not merely an incidental feature of Christianity, like candles in churches or stained-glass windows; it was an essential characteristic of the religion. Chastity or sexual restraint was an ideal that lay very near the center of Christianity. It lay closer to the center for Catholicism (with its monasticism and celibate priesthood) than for Protestantism, but Protestantism was far, far from being sexually permissive. For nearly two thousand years a sexually liberated Christianity had been a contradiction in terms. And so if you participated in the sexual revolution you were, either intentionally or not, and either wittingly or not, participating in a great attack on Christianity.

If you had participated in the earlier great attacks on Christianity, the deistic attack or the agnostic attack, you would have had to take a somewhat intellectual approach; you would have had to familiarize yourself with the arguments of Voltaire or Tom Paine, the arguments of Darwin or Herbert Spencer; you might even have had to read a few books. Not so with the sexual revolution. Intellectually speaking, it was much easier. In this case all you had to do was go to bed with your boyfriend or girlfriend, and after the sexual act was finished congratulate yourself on being brave and progressive. As for arguments, you needed nothing more sophisticated than this: "How does it harm anybody if my girlfriend and I have sex—consensual sex with precautions being taken with regard to pregnancy and disease?"

The sexual revolution that began in the 1960s, and in many respects continues to this day, is part of a much larger phenomenon, namely modern-day atheism. Let us call this modern-day atheism "secular humanism." I use this expression out of courtesy to our modern atheists. For the word "atheism" is a purely negative word, an indication of mere disbelief in God. The expression "secular humanism" is more positive, indicating not just disbelief in God but certain pro-humanity values—and this value above all: the right of individual humans to be free, to be morally autonomous, to be self-governing. Since, according to Christian theology, God is the only truly free being, this atheistic desire for autonomy is tantamount to a desire that individual humans be godlike. Although sexual freedom is not the only kind of freedom believed in by secular humanists, it is a very important kind, perhaps the single most important kind. In any case, it is restrictions on sexual freedom that most easily rouse the irritation and anger of secular humanists. Indeed, it provokes their righteous indignation. As sexual restraint has been an essential element of traditional Christianity, so sexual freedom is an essential element of secular humanism.

Not all atheism involves the advocacy of sexual freedom. Take for example the atheism of the ancient philosopher Epicurus (c. 340–270 BC). He did not advise his followers to live a sexually free life; on the contrary, he recommended sexual restraint; for a lack of sexual restraint could lead to a loss of what Epicurus saw as life's greatest pleasure, peace of mind. Further, the atheism of Epicurus was not intended as an attack Christianity, for he lived a few centuries before Christianity appeared in the world. By contrast, today's secular humanists *are* trying to attack Christianity, and their advocacy of sexual freedom is an important element of that attack. That, it seems to me, is the real point of modern-day sexual freedom—to get rid of that hated thing, Christianity.

In the heyday of the communist revolution in Russia, atheistic communists tried to get rid of Christianity by violent means, e.g., by shooting priests and monks and nuns, and by tearing down churches and monasteries, and by banning religious schools. Our secular humanists are smarter than the old communists. To date they have avoided violence. Instead they use the seductive means of a virtually unlimited sexual freedom. Get a Christian (or potential Christian) to approve of sexual liberty, and there's a good chance that you'll be able to draw that person away from Christianity and in the direction of agnosticism or even atheism.

෨෬ ෬෨

But this sexual freedom advocated by secular humanists and other champions of the sexual revolution is not perfectly unlimited. At least three sexual activities are considered wrong: rape (or coerced sex), sex between adults and children, and adultery (or other kinds of sexual infidelity). By contrast, heterosexual or homosexual sex between unmarried consenting adults is considered to be morally quite okay.

In connection with these three forbidden activities, a few points should be noted. For one, the line between rape and consensual sex is not always clear. What at first glance appears to be consensual sex may not, upon further consideration, be truly consensual; or it may seem consensual to one partner, non-consensual to the other. Even when there is no physical coercion, there may be psychological coercion; or the "victim" may have recently had a bit too much to drink and therefore, while under the influence, may not have been able to give genuine consent. It frequently happens on college campuses that a young woman (almost never a young man) concludes the next day that the sexual intercourse she had last night wasn't truly consensual; she was pressured, or she was half-drunk, and therefore, she concludes, she was the victim of rape (so-called "date rape").

For another, while it is almost[2] universally held by those who subscribe to the modern sex ethic that it is wrong for an adult to have sex with a child, there is no agreement as to where the line is to be drawn between childhood and adulthood. When does a boy or girl cease to be a child and therefore become eligible for sexual relations with an adult? Some people say it's at the age of eighteen. Others say it is sixteen. Still others say it depends on the psychological and physical maturity of the younger partner; some kids are ready for sex at thirteen, others aren't ready until they're twenty-one, while some people are never mature enough to handle sex. Many say that everything depends on the age gap between the

2. Almost but not quite—for there are at least a few advocates of adult-child sex.

older and the younger partner; that what would be allowable when there is a gap of two or three years (e.g., one partner sixteen, the other nineteen) would be quite unallowable when the gap is ten or twenty years.

Again, while adultery/infidelity is generally considered to be wrong, sexual libertarians allow for exceptions. It is not considered wrong if it is an instance of consensual infidelity; that is, if it is done with the permission, either express or implied, of the spouse/ partner of the unfaithful person. And since the wrongness of infidelity, according to the modern sex ethic, consists of the pain, or at least the serious risk of pain, that the infidelity inflicts on the innocent partner, adherents of the modern ethic will often argue that infidelity is not wrong, or only minimally wrong, if it is managed in such a way that the pain is zero and the risk of pain is very close to zero. In other words, infidelity is not wrong if you do it in a very careful way; just be sure that your partner suspects nothing, and so he/she will suffer no harm. Other adherents of the modern ethic won't allow for this "be very careful" exception. They say it's unrealistic. They can point out that prisons a filled with people who ahead of time were sure that they were committing the "perfect crime." Likewise, the "perfect act of infidelity" is an exceedingly rare thing. Therefore it shouldn't be attempted. Still others say that, while there is nothing intrinsically wrong about a well-concealed act of infidelity, such concealment necessarily involves lying; and lying is wrong; and therefore infidelity is wrong. In short, though sexual liberationists tend to agree with the general principle that adultery/infidelity is wrong, they are far from agreement as to exceptions to this rule.

However, apart from these three exceptions (rape, child molestation, and infidelity), anything goes.

The theoretical justification for this ethic of sexual freedom derives from what is very probably the dominant theory of morality in America today, especially dominant among the younger generations. I mean a theory that may be called *moral liberalism*, which comprises two fundamental principles: (a) the *personal liberty principle* (PLP) and (b) the *tolerance principle* (TP).

a. According to the PLP an action is morally permissible provided it does no harm to another person. To understand what this means, a few clarifications are needed.

- The harm in question may be any of four kinds:

    - Physical harm: for example, murder, rape, a punch in the nose.

    - Harm to property: for example, fraud, theft, arson, vandalism.

    - Reputational harm: for example, libel, slander.

    - Emotional harm: for example, emotional abuse, the infliction of needless emotional pain.

- The harm in question must be a secular, tangible harm. For instance, it is wrong to steal a dollar from a Muslim, but not wrong to persuade him to eat pork, nor is it wrong to persuade a Christian to blaspheme.

- The harm in question must be clearly evident, not merely speculative. If the harm will happen, not today, but ten or fifty or a hundred years down the road, this consequence must be scientifically demonstrable.

- The harm in question doesn't count as harm when the harmed person gives his or her antecedent consent. For instance, a surgery patient gives permission to a surgeon to cut the patient open. Again, in a consensual sadomasochistic relationship, the masochist gives his sadistic partner permission to inflict pain on him.

- The harm in question is harm to non-consenting *others*; it is not harm to the actor himself. If it sometimes appears that certain actions are prohibited in order to protect the performer of that action (e.g., bans on smoking cigarettes), these bans and requirements are normally justified by moral liberals in terms of the protection of others (e.g., protecting others from secondhand smoke).

- This freedom applies only to adults who are of sound mind. It doesn't apply to insane persons or to children—though here again there is no agreement as to where childhood ends and adulthood begins.

b. The TP is simply the other side of the PLP coin. It says: We must be tolerant of any and all conduct of others provided this conduct does no harm to another person.

If moral liberalism is, as I think it is, the prevailing theory of morality in America, it follows that our sex ethic will be highly permissive. For as long as your sexual conduct does no harm to others (according to the concept of "harm" outlined above), there is no reason you shouldn't do whatever you like in the way of sexual conduct and no reason you should disapprove of others who do whatever *they* like in the way of sexual conduct.

I don't mean to suggest that the theory of moral liberalism came first and our highly permissive sex ethic came later as a deduction from this theory. I doubt it happened that way. I think the ethic of sex freedom came first, and the theory of moral liberalism came later as a way to justify the ethic of sexual freedom. But once this ethical theory had been adopted, it not only justified the sexual freedom that had already emerged; it suggested and inspired more radical notions of sex freedom.

It is unnecessary, I suppose, to point out that the theory of moral liberalism is quite a different thing from the Christian theory of morality, based as the latter is on the Ten Commandments, the Beatitudes, and above all the example of Jesus Christ.

⌇⌇⌇

If we accept the theory of moral liberalism, as described above, we have no grounds for disapproving of many very un-Christian sexual practices that are common in American today. These common practices include:

- Fornication.

- Cohabitation between unmarried sex partners.

- Homosexual practice.

- Same-sex marriage.

- Abortion.

There is, however, something of a problem with the last item on this list, abortion. Those who defend abortion argue that it, like fornication, homosexuality, etc., does no harm to anybody; and if it does no harm, it is not morally wrong. But at first glance abortion seems to do serious harm to somebody, namely the unborn baby. Very serious harm indeed, for it kills the baby. What harm could be more serious than that? Abortion appears quite plainly to be a kind of homicide.

Now, this appearance of homicide is an embarrassment for those who defend what they say is a right—a fundamental human right—to abortion. And so they have come up with a number of arguments (very shabby arguments, it seems to me) to "prove" that abortion is not homicide; or to prove that, if it is homicide, it is warranted homicide. A list of these arguments is given below. It is not necessarily a complete list; for if you are a pro-abortion person and I can persuade you to drop *all* the following arguments, you will almost certainly find a new argument to justify abortion.

- The entity killed in an abortion is not a human being.

- The entity killed in an abortion is only a "potential" human being.

- The entity killed in an abortion is a human being, but it is not a *person*; and it is wrong to kill a human being only when that human is a person.

- The entity killed in an abortion is, at least for the first few months, too *small* to be a human being; no bigger than a peanut.

- The entity killed in an abortion is part of the woman's body, not an independent thing.

- The entity killed in an abortion is, at least early in the pregnancy, an unformed mass of tissue; it is not an organized substance.

- The entity killed in an abortion is of no value unless somebody values it. Obviously its "mother" doesn't value it; otherwise she wouldn't be killing it; and it is as yet too young and undeveloped to value itself.

- The entity killed in an abortion has no right to inhabit the mother's body, any more than a home invader has a right to take up uninvited residence in your house for nine months or so.

- The entity killed in an abortion is an "unjust aggressor" attacking the mother, and therefore may be lawfully killed the way we may lawfully kill somebody trying to murder us or the way we may kill an enemy combatant in warfare.

- A woman who gets rid of an "unwanted" unborn baby is doing the child a favor; for what fate could be worse than being an unwanted child? It's better never to have been born.

- If the fetus has a right to life, the woman carrying the fetus has an even stronger right not to give birth to an unwanted child, and the latter rights trumps the former.

- Those who disapprove of abortion are simply trying to restrict the sexual freedom of women and the freedom of women generally.

- Those who oppose abortion call themselves, very hypocritically, "pro-life"—which they are not, for they don't care about the life of humans who have actually been born, e.g., poor people, minorities, death row convicts.

- Those who disapprove of abortion are misogynists.

- Those who disapprove of abortion are deficient in compassion.

- Those who disapprove of abortion are religious fanatics who wish to turn American from a democracy into a theocracy.

- A woman has a right to "control" her own body; the right to a woman's bodily autonomy trumps any so-called "right to life" a fetus may have.[3]

- Those who disapprove of abortion are for the most part vulgar, uneducated, and from the lower classes; whereas we who approve of it are for the most part well-mannered, well-educated, and from the higher classes. In disputes between Ivy League graduates and those who have not gone beyond high school or a community college, the Ivy Leaguers are always right.

All these are philosophically worthless arguments, as any intelligent person should be able to see. But it doesn't matter from the point of view of those who believe in abortion rights. For they feel they must have a legal right to abortion if they are to protect and preserve their moral regime of nearly unlimited sexual freedom. In such a regime, "accidents" will happen. Despite all the pills and condoms in the world, girls and women will from time to time become unintentionally pregnant. Some relatively handy way will have to be found of getting rid of these accidents. If abortion is not readily available, a regime of sexual freedom becomes risky; a "chilling effect" is placed on the modern sex ethic. And if a hundred pro-abortion arguments are shot down as fallacious, we pro-abortion folks will just have to come up with a hundred-and-first argument.

⁓⁓

If the theory of moral liberalism provides a moral justification for the five forms of conduct itemized above (fornication, unmarried cohabitation, homosexuality, same-sex marriage, abortion), it also provides a justification for the following practices—practices that are not, or at least not yet, widely approved of.

- Polygamy.

---

3. At the time I'm writing this book, 2022, this "bodily autonomy" argument is probably the most popular argument offered in defense of abortion—or at least it was until those who oppose COVID vaccinations began using the very same "bodily autonomy" arguments.

- Polyamory.

- Open marriage.

- Group marriage.

- Incestuous relations between adults (provided precautions are taken to prevent pregnancy).

- Sex with animals.

- Necrophilia (provided the "owner" of the corpse has no objection).

- Sado-masochism.

- Dueling.

- Gladiator fights.

- Human sacrifice (provided the person being sacrificed is an adult volunteer).

- Infanticide.

- Voluntary euthanasia.

- In some circumstances, involuntary euthanasia.

- Coprophagia.

I'm not saying that all of these, or even any of them, are about to become fashionable. I'm just saying that they follow logically from the idea of moral liberalism. If moral liberalism is a sound theory of morality, all of the above are morally permissible, for none of them causes harm to a nonconsenting other person. Or to put this more correctly: While these activities seem to morally conservative person (like the author of this book) to be very harmful, they don't count as harmful when judged by the idea of harm usually used by moral liberals.

Some of the hypothetical practices itemized above are, I think, unlikely ever to be widely accepted. Sex with animals, for instance. I can imagine that some Oprah-like afternoon TV program might feature a man who has sex with his dog and might present this man-dog relationship in a way that tugs on our sympathetic heartstrings. All the same, I think the audience will be far more likely to feel disgust than to feel than to feel sympathy. The "argument from disgust" will be stronger than the "argument from sympathy."

But then again, I remember the now-long-ago days when I was a young philosophy professor. To stimulate a discussion I would sometimes ask my class, "What's wrong with homosexuality?" And the common answer was, "It's disgusting." Well, a half-century later it is apparently no longer disgusting to many people, especially younger people. So not-disgusting is it that most Americans now approve of homosexuality and same-sex marriage. Could it be then that our reactions of disgust will continue to change so that before the end of the present century we will no longer feel disgust at the thought of a man having sex with a dog or a goat? I don't think so. And I certainly hope not. But who can be sure?

And I am even more confident that we will continue be disgusted by the thought of coprophagia, no matter how much compassion we may feel for a man (or woman) who engages in this unspeakably disgusting (not to mention very unhealthy) practice.

But some of the absurdities listed above are likely, I fear, to become widely accepted. When I say "widely accepted" I don't mean widely practiced. I mean that many people, perhaps the majority of the American public, while unwilling to engage in these practices themselves, will cease to disapprove of them when engaged in by others. They will be morally tolerant. I'm thinking of consensual adultery (open marriage), polygamy, polyamory, and group marriage. Even now many people engage in these practices, and almost nobody who subscribes to the theory of moral liberalism seriously objects. How can they object? For if moral liberalism is right, then it follows that these practices are right. Those who approve are simply being logical. They are drawing conclusions that follow from their moral liberalism premises.

I think eventually, once these adulterous practices are widely accepted, an acceptance of adult incest will follow; that is, adult incest with the proviso that precautions be taken so that these incestuous relations don't lead to the birth of children. This proviso will have to be added in order to deal with the objection that there is an increased chance that children born of incestuous unions will be physically or mentally defective in some serious way.

I also expect that, given society's support for the theory of moral liberalism, euthanasia will before long be accepted. Its acceptance will come about in stages. (a) First will come physician-assisted suicide, wherein the physician provides the lethal drug but does not administer it. (b) Next will come voluntary euthanasia, wherein the physician (or somebody else, a friend or a family member) actually administers the lethal drug at the request of, or at least with the consent of, the patient. (c) Then will come "presumptively voluntary" euthanasia, wherein it is presumed by a trustee that the patient, who is no longer capable of making a decision (because of a coma or other disabling condition), would, if he were capable, chose to be put to death. (d) After this will come involuntary euthanasia, wherein the patient, without giving consent, and without presumptive consent, is killed because we believe that he/she would be better off dead. (e) After this comes social wellbeing euthanasia, wherein the patient is put to death because it is believed that persons other than the patient (e.g., family, friends, society at large) will be better off when the patient is dead.

But what about dueling? And gladiator fights? And human sacrifice? Will they ever be widely accepted? I find it hard to imagine that they will be. But not so many years ago I found it hard to imagine that same-sex marriage would ever be accepted. I was wrong. I may be wrong about these things too.

Of course, in predicting the future of all these logical deductions from the principle of moral liberalism, I'm assuming that there will be no significant revival of Christian morality in the United States. I'm assuming that moral liberalism, even now the dominant moral theory in the USA, will grow stronger and stronger, relatively unimpeded by an ever-weakening Christianity. However, if there is (as I and many others hope) a revival of Christianity, my predictions will (thank God) turn out to be in error.

13

The Liberal Response to the Sexual Revolution

AN EARLY SIGN OF the way liberal Protestantism would respond to the sexual revolution came with the publication in 1966 of Joseph Fletcher's book, *Situation Ethics: the New Morality*. Fletcher,[1] an ordained Episcopal minister[2] who was at the time the professor of social ethics at the Episcopal Theology School (in Cambridge, MA, right next door to Harvard University), argued that for Christians there is only one exceptionless moral norm, one absolute moral rule: namely, the love-your-neighbor rule. All other rules (e.g., "Don't steal," "Don't lie," "Don't commit adultery") are only

---

1. I once briefly met Fletcher in 1968 at a cocktail party closing a philosophical conference in Washington, DC. He was a friendly old guy. I liked him. I got the impression that he was the kind of man it was hard not to like. It didn't occur to me at the time that he was a man striking a lethal blow at the Protestant Consensus.

2. Later in life he became an atheist. He was one of the signers of the *Humanist Manifesto II*, an atheistic proclamation. And he later served as president from 1974 to 1976 of the Euthanasia Society of America (See Wikipedia, "Joseph Fletcher.").

relative, not absolute. At any moment they may be trumped by the supreme rule, the rule of love.

Fletcher didn't restrict himself to questions of sexual morality. However, given that the book was written in the mid-1960s, just as the sexual revolution was beginning to sweep the country, my guess is that the potential application of Fletcher's argument to questions of sexual morality is what made the book something of a theological best-seller.

One of the illustrative examples he gives in the book has to do with a German woman who at the end of World War II was being held prisoner in a Russian camp. Back in Berlin her husband and children were looking for her. The German woman felt she had a duty to return to her husband and children. Now, it so happened that the Russians were releasing pregnant women from the camp. A friendly guard at the camp helped her by having sexual intercourse with her, thereby making her pregnant. Accordingly, she was released. Her husband and children were delighted when she returned home, and they had no objection to her adultery, for it was motivated by love—not love of the Russian guard but love of her family. The moral of the story is this: while the commandment against adultery is generally applicable, there are exceptions—and not just for German women in Russian camps.

This principle—what we may call "the Fletcher principle"—has since then been utilized by liberal Protestant theologians, ministers, and lay persons to justify Christian acceptance of many of the aspects of the sexual revolution. Many sexual acts that Christians have traditionally regarded as forbidden are, it turns out, allowable provided they are done from love. By "love" Fletcher meant not a mere feeling but conduct likely to bring about good consequences. Though he didn't call himself such, Fletcher was a utilitarian, a de facto follower of Jeremy Bentham.

Christianity has been in the world for about twenty centuries; but according to modern liberal Protestantism, it was only late in the twentieth century that Christians first understood what Jesus really meant when he said that we must love one another. Jesus meant that love of neighbor is the one and only absolute commandment; all the others, all the more narrow and more specific commandments, are only relative. Every single one of the specific commandments may be dispensed with depending on circumstances. They are rules of thumb, not categorical imperatives.

Another writer who made a considerable contribution to the advance of liberal Protestantism during the era of the sexual revolution was John Shelby Spong (1931–2021), once the Episcopal bishop of Newark, New Jersey. In his retirement Spong was a prolific writer, and most of this writing has served to undermine belief in traditional Christian doctrine and morality. Spong says that he believes in God, but that the God he believes in is a "non-theistic" God—whatever that can mean; for it sounds rather like saying that one believes in non-circular circles. He greatly admires Jesus, who was a very good and wise man—even though he was not God, was not born of a virgin, did not rise from the dead, and is not our Lord and Savior. Spong has written a series of books and delivered hundreds of lectures, both in the USA and elsewhere, devoted to the demolition of classical Christian doctrines. For the most part his books have sold well (Spong has a felicitous prose style) and his lectures have been well-attended, for there is a great potential audience in the world looking for reasons to drop belief in Christian doctrine and morals while at the same time continuing to call oneself a Christian.[3] If you're looking for Christian reasons for ceasing to believe in Christianity, Spong is your man. He has made it clear that he doesn't believe in a single article of the Nicene Creed, except possibly (just possibly) belief in something that may be called "God."

Yet he calls himself a Christian—a believer in a new and improved kind of Christianity.

Needless to say, Spong has endorsed the sexual revolution; that is to say, he has provided Christian justifications for fornication, unmarried cohabitation, abortion, and homosexuality—not

---

3. I heard him speak once, a few summers ago at Chautauqua, New York. He was a charming speaker.

to mention justifications for euthanasia. Let's look at his 1988 book: *Living in Sin: A Bishop Rethinks Human Sexuality.*

Early in his book Spong lays down two premises that will inform everything that follows. First, Christianity is, or at least it should be, an *inclusive* religion. God is the God of *all* people, not just Christians and Jews, not just males, not just heterosexuals, not just people who systematically abstain from what Christianity has traditionally called sexual sin—but *everybody.* A new and improved Christianity will have to see itself as a religion for *all* people. Second, until just the other day (so to speak) women, who make up half the human race, have been regarded as inferior human beings, second-class persons, not entitled to the rights and freedoms that the other half, men, have traditionally been entitled to, including sexual rights and freedoms. We are now living in a new human era, the era of gender equality. In our modern world women are the legal and social equals of men, and, thanks to readily available birth control, they are rapidly becoming the sexual equals too. A new and improved Christianity will have to recognize these facts and will therefore have to treat women as being just as fully human as men, and as being just as fully as men in possession of sexual rights.

Spong has a number of recommendations for a new and improved Christian sexual morality. He doesn't seem to notice that he gets these new ideas not from the Bible, but from secular humanists who promote an anti-Biblical sexual morality.

1. A new and improved Christianity will have to recognize that an antique code of sexual morality that demanded premarital abstention from sexual love makes sense no longer. Once upon a time boys and girls got married in their late teens. Now typical young persons don't get married until well into their twenties or even thirties. It is unrealistic and unreasonable to expect them to deprive themselves of sexual love until that late date. Christianity, if it is to remain relevant in the modern world, will have to adjust to the facts of the modern world.

2. Again, Christianity used to take it for granted that marriage was a lifelong thing. While lifelong monogamy may be an ideal, it is no longer a *practical* ideal for great numbers of persons. In the modern world many marriages break up, and the people who get divorced often marry new partners. While this is often a sad event for the couple in question, it is a common fact in modern life, and the church, instead counting this fact as a sin, must do its best to help such people through their transition.

3. Nowadays many older people whose marriage has come to an end either by death or by divorce feel a need for sexual companionship while at the same time, for a variety of good reasons, they do not wish to marry. The church, instead of denouncing these nonmarital unions as sinful, must bless them.

4. Further, while the church, in its ignorance and prejudice, traditionally condemned homosexuality and homosexual relationships, today, thanks to the enlightenment provided by modern science and psychology, we know that gays and lesbians are born that way; and the church, instead of condemning these relationships, must bless them.

In sum, Spong suggests that the church, which has always blessed marriage, must devise ceremonies to bless premarital cohabitation, to bless divorce, to bless post-marital sexual relationships, and to bless homosexual relationships. Rather oddly, he makes no proposal to bless polygamous relationships; he seems to expect that couples involved in these nontraditional sexual relationships will be monogamous. Nor does he propose blessings for adulterous relationships. He believes that persons involved in these nontraditional relationships should be faithful to their partners; he seems not to suspect that a rejection of old-fashioned Christian sexual morality will encourage widespread adultery.

As for passages in the Bible that condemn premarital, post-marital, and homosexual relationships, Spong explains them away. He says that if you read the Bible carefully and if you understand the social, economic, and historical circumstances in which these

Biblical condemnations were formulated, you will see either (a) that these Biblical passages don't mean what we have traditionally thought they meant (for example, the great sin of Sodom, says Spong, wasn't sodomy, it was lack of hospitality), or (b) that Biblical condemnations don't apply today, in a world radically changed from the ancient world.

You may wonder why Spong, who rejects many old and great doctrines of Christianity (for example, the divinity of Christ, the virgin birth, the resurrection, and perhaps even the existence of God [remember that Spong says the God he believes in is a "non-theistic" God]), and rejects Christian sexual morality, calls himself a Christian. I wonder too. In fact he is not a Christian if the word "Christian" has any stable meaning. Rather, he is a splendid example of how far liberal Protestantism will go in in its efforts to cling to the name "Christian" while tossing overboard almost all the content of Christianity.

അ∞ ∞ə

Liberal Protestantism has responded to the sexual revolution in essentially the same way it had responded to those earlier great attacks on Christianity, the deistic and agnostic attacks. Those earlier responses, remember, had four steps:

1. An acknowledgement that the anti-Christian critique had some merit.

2. A refusal to agree with the critics that Christianity should be abandoned.

3. An attempt to blend the best of Christianity with the best of the criticism.

4. A doubling down on the moral element in religion.

So let us look at how liberal Protestantism has gone through these four steps in its response to the sexual revolution.

The Anti-Christians Make Some Good Points

The sexual revolution, with its disdain for traditional sexual moral-ity, led liberal Protestants to admit that historical Christianity had focused excessively on sexual purity, as though that is the heart of Christianity. But it isn't. Love is the heart of Christianity.

For centuries, however, there had been some excuse for this undue stress on chastity, not charity. After all, those were centu-ries in which birth control wasn't available for the masses, and an unmarried pregnancy could be disastrous for the mother and the fatherless child. So there had to be a strict rule banning premarital sex; and when that rule was violated and a girl became pregnant, there had to be a backup rule that required the father to marry the mother prior to birth of the child. And divorce, except in the rarest of instances, had to be banned; otherwise men would be free to abandon their wives and children, who, without the sup-port of husbands and fathers, would find themselves in a terrible socio-economic situation. And adultery couldn't be regarded as a relatively easy-to-pardon offense; for it too, given the social reali-ties of the time, could be disastrous for all parties concerned. As for homosexual behavior—though it may have been as common in the old days as it is today, it could not be condoned. For if you said that homosexuality, that quite extreme deviation from the Chris-tian ideal of marital sex, is okay, how could you tell young people that fornication, a far milder deviation, is grievously wrong?

But those were the old days, and the old days are no more. Effective contraception is now readily available; more so than ever now that "the pill" has been invented. Premarital sex, provided it is done with contraception and between partners whose relationship is mutually respectful and affectionate, is a harmless activity; and even when it doesn't lead to marriage between that particular cou-ple, it may well help them in their growth toward psycho-sexual maturity. Divorce-and-remarriage is a far more manageable thing in the modern world than it would have been centuries ago. Adul-tery is still wrong; but it no longer has the tremendous potential for harm that it had in earlier times. It is no longer the enormous sin it once was; it is now a normal-size sin, often even a small sin. As for homosexuality—a disposition to it seems to be innate in some people; probably something genetic. If so, doesn't that mean that homosexual intercourse is normal or natural for persons who are born that way (provided of course that homosexual partners treat one another with respect and affection, and take precautions against disease)? Doesn't it mean that God, their Maker, intended homosexual persons to engage in same-sex lovemaking?[4]

In sum, liberal Protestants acknowledged that the sexual revolution was correct when it criticized Christianity for its sexual puritanism.

Let's Not Give Up Christianity

But, said liberal Protestants, the sexual revolutionaries are wrong, terribly wrong, when they say, as many of them do, that Christianity is an out-of-date religion; that it needs to be given up. Wrong, very wrong, said liberal Protestants. Christianity is a beautiful religion. It has imperfections, we grant that. But the history of Christianity is a history of improvement; it is a history of the gradual shedding of its imperfections. Think of the Reformation. What was that but a great shedding of Christian imperfections? And think of the Protestant modernism of people like Harry Emerson Fosdick. What was that but a great shedding of the Christian imperfections embraced by fundamentalists? The church will always be in need of reform, and as it reforms it will move closer and closer to Christian perfection—even though it will never fully arrive. At the moment the reform we need is a reform in our sexual morality—and we thank the sexual revolution, which is perhaps a thing of atheistic provenance, for having reminded us of that, even though we cannot go along with the atheistic demand that we abandon Christianity.

---

4. These were common liberal thoughts prior to the emergence of the AIDS epidemic in the 1980s. After that point, liberal Protestants stressed that homosexuals have a moral duty to protect themselves and their partners from disease.

In this our latest reform, our shedding of sexual puritanism, we are not doing a purely negative thing, any more than Michelangelo did a purely negative thing when he chipped away at the block of marble that would become his great statue of David. No, the sculptor's chipping away reveals the great beauty of that which is hidden underneath. Likewise when we free Christianity from its undue puritanism we reveal more clearly what was hidden beneath, the magnificent ethic of love preached by Jesus and exemplified in his life and his tragic death.

Blending the Best of Christianity with the Best of Anti-Christianity

It is often said that Thomas Aquinas, by embracing the philosophy of Aristotle and blending it with Christian doctrine, "Christianized" or "baptized" Aristotle. Similarly liberal Protestants can say that they "Christianized" or "baptized" the sexual revolution by embracing it. And by virtue of their synthesis of Christianity and the sexual revolution they believe they have improved both Christianity and the sexual revolution.

The great fault of the sexual revolution in its purely secular form, liberal Protestants argue, is that it tolerates any and every kind of sexual relationship between consenting adults even if this relationship is casual, uncaring, selfish, and virtually animalistic. This is wrong. From a Christian point of view acts of sexual intercourse, whether married or unmarried and whether homosexual or heterosexual, should be based on an underlying relationship that is respectful and loving. When liberal Protestants say that it must be "loving," they don't necessarily mean that word in a merely romantic sense; they mean it in a Christians sense; they mean it in the sense that Jesus meant it when he said we must love our neighbors. We must wish to benefit our neighbors. Jesus illustrated the idea of Christian love with the story of the good Samaritan. The Samaritan wished to do something significantly good for the injured man. Thus should it be with sexual intercourse done in the spirit of Christian love. The partners should aim not simply at having fun (though there is nothing wrong with having fun), but at conferring genuine benefits upon one another. They should do this in the case of a lifelong married relationship, and they should do it in the case of a one-night stand (the relationship, remember, between the Samaritan and the injured man was a one-night thing). At the same time they should remember that sex done in a spirit of Christian love is far more likely in a lifelong marriage than in a one-night stand.

And thus liberal Protestants have been able to give their stamp of moral approval to fornication, unmarried sexual cohabitation, adultery (in some circumstances), divorce-and-remarriage, homosexual practice, same-sex marriage, and—something that is far from being a minor part of the Christian sexual revolution— the ordination of gay/lesbian/transgender clergypersons.

They have also given their stamp of approval to abortion. While some liberal Protestants (especially female clergy who happen to be ardent feminists or lesbians) have given enthusiastic approval to abortion, many liberal Protestants have found it uncomfortable to give this approval since abortion appears to be a form of homicide. But if you give your approval to a moral regime of sexual freedom, it is impossible, at least if you are a logical person, to disapprove of abortion. For "accidents" will happen, and girls and women will sometimes become pregnant contrary to their wishes. If abortion is not legally available to correct these "accidents," sexual freedom will become a risky thing. It will suffer a "chilling effect." And so liberal Protestants have generally given their approval, though somewhat reluctantly, to the legality of abortion. They are not, they will tell you, pro-abortion—meaning that they (that is, most of them) do not personally like it and would not personally take part in an abortion. "We dislike it," they will often say. "But we think it has to be legal in all cases to make sure we can take care of the hard cases." Liberal Protestants will rarely applaud abortions done in a casual or thoughtless way. The woman having an abortion should think long and hard about it, should (if she's a church-going person) consult her pastor, and should do it from motives of Christian love: love for herself, for her boyfriend or husband, for her family and friends, and (above all) for the "baby" she's killing. A Christian abortion is an abortion done in a spirit of Christian love. You kill your unborn baby out of love; you want to spare the little thing the misery of living as an unwanted child. Jesus would approve.

Doubling Down on the Moral Element of Religion

I have said that liberal Protestantism, while dropping elements of Christian doctrine, compensates for this by putting a very strong emphasis on the moral content of Christianity. However, this is not necessarily the same moral content that was familiar to the early church fathers (e.g. Tertullian, Augustine, Jerome), or to the medieval theologians (e.g., Anselm, Thomas Aquinas), or to the Reformers (e.g., Luther, Calvin), or to the great American revivalist preachers (e.g., Jonathan Edwards, Charles Finney, Billy Graham). Our latest and most up-to-date liberal Protestants are strongly moralistic, and their moralism, they tell us, is based on one great Christian commandment: *love your neighbor*. At first hearing, that sounds pretty traditional and orthodox. But when reduced to specific sub-commandments, this becomes something that would shock and appall Tertullian, Augustine, Anselm, Aquinas, Luther, Calvin, Edwards, Finney, and Billy Graham—not to mention Jesus and Paul. Among other things, the commandment of love as understood by liberal Protestants allows, indeed usually commands, the following.

- Ordain practicing homosexuals to the ministry.
- Perform gay weddings in church.
- Support a legal right to abortion.
- Resist attempts to restrict abortion rights in any way.
- Support transgenderism.
- Oppose attempts to reverse or weaken Roe v. Wade (the famous abortion ruling).

- Oppose attempts to reverse Obergefell v. Hodges (the same-sex marriage ruling).

- Support Planned Parenthood and its abortion agenda.

- Vote for political candidates who are pro-abortion and pro-same-sex marriage and pro-transgenderism.

All of the above are of course items on the political agenda of secular humanists. In general, liberal Protestants lean in the same direction as secular humanists, and not just on matters having to do with sex. And so, just as secular humanists are "social justice warriors," so liberal Protestants tend to be social justice warriors. And so, just as secular humanists are especially concerned with the oppression (or alleged oppression) of certain demographic groups (e.g., women, homosexuals, transgenders, African Americans, other persons of color, political refugees, Muslims, and poor people), so liberal Protestants tend to be especially concerned with precisely these same groups. However, liberal Protestants usually become concerned with the unfortunate situation of these groups only a few years after secular humanists have launched their own concern. For it is not until secular humanists have decided what they think about this or that political question that liberal Protestants discover what they themselves should think—and lo and behold! they think the same thing as do secular humanists. Even though many liberal Protestants imagine that they derive their moral and political values from Jesus and Paul and the Bible, in fact they derive these values from secular humanism. They are far more likely to be guided by the ACLU or by NARAL than by the New Testament.

☙ ❧

But since this chapter is concerned with the sexual revolution, and not these other questions, I will stop here, not pursuing social justice issues. I will only add, by way of summing up, that liberal Protestantism in its latest form is barely distinguishable from secular humanism. Liberal Protestants nowadays have very few ideas or values of their own; for the most part they borrow their ideas and values from secular humanism. At this point, more than two hundred years after it began about 1800 with the Unitarians of Boston, liberal Protestantism is little more than secular humanism (a kind of atheism) with some Christian fairy dust sprinkled on it.

14

Evangelical Response to the Sexual Revolution

OVER THE CENTURIES AMERICAN Protestantism has blown hot and cold over the question of whether or not the power of government should be used to promote Christianity and a Christian way of life. In seventeenth-century Massachusetts there was a theoretical separation of church and state. Minsters did not hold political office, and political figures did not govern the church—at least not *qua* political figures, even though they might play an important governing role *qua* pious lay persons. But it was taken for granted that everybody living in a particular small town or living in a particular parish in a bigger place like Boston would be a member of the local congregation, and would attend church on Sunday and listen to the edifying sermons delivered therein. And it was further taken for granted that both ministers and politicians, though operating in distinct spheres, would be dedicated to the advancement of Christianity: this would be the main responsibility of the ministers, a secondary responsibility of the politicians.

Even that early, however, there were a few dissenters. Roger Williams, the founder of Rhode Island, was expelled from

Massachusetts because of his teaching that the body politic should allow religious freedom to unorthodox (or unconventional) Protestants and even to non-Protestants; to Catholics, Jews, Muslims, atheists, and so on.

Some of the thirteen colonies had a system of established churches. In Massachusetts, for a few decades following American independence, the Congregational Church was the official taxpayer-supported church, and later, following the split between Congregationalists and Unitarians, the Unitarian Church became a second official or established church.

When the United States was created, however, it was unthinkable that there should be a national established church—unthinkable partly because there were some very influential persons (e.g., Jefferson and Madison) who had a strong theoretical commitment to religious liberty, but even more so because of the tremendous ecclesiastic diversity in America. There were Congregationalists, Presbyterians, Unitarians, Universalists, Anglicans, Baptists, Methodists, Lutherans, Dutch Reformed, Catholics, Jews, deists, and a few others, not to mention the religiously indifferent people. Practically speaking, there was no way an official or established national church could be imposed on so ecclesiastically diverse a population.

And so the new USA became committed to religious liberty, and almost all Protestants were happy with this commitment. This commitment was enshrined in the First Amendment to the Constitution. And it was neatly, if not altogether accurately,[1] summarized in Jefferson's phrase about a "wall of separation" between church and state.

Despite this commitment, however, and despite the unwillingness of American governments, whether local or state or federal, to give legal sanction to doctrinal beliefs, the states of the USA generally had a system of legal prohibitions based on the customary morality of the people, and this customary morality was

1. When I say "not altogether accurately," I have in mind that the First Amendment tells the political regime to keep its nose out of church affairs and its hands off the religious conscience of believers, but it does not tell religious believers that their political views and actions may not be inspired by religious beliefs.

Protestant morality. Consequently, the production or distribution of obscenity/pornography was banned almost everywhere, and homosexual conduct was a criminal offense in every state. And divorce, though allowable in certain circumstances, was not easily obtained; it was not until after the Civil War that divorce became relatively common in the USA. Someone might have argued that this enforcement of Christian morality by the government was a violation of the principle of church-state separation; but rarely or never was it so argued.

※ ※

In the nineteenth century conservative Protestants persuaded the government to ban Sunday delivery of the mail, a sin against the Sabbath. Beginning in the nineteenth century and culminating in the early twentieth, Protestants, mostly conservative, made an even greater attempt to enlist government in an attempt to lead the nation in the direction of Christian virtue. That is, they championed enactment of the Eighteenth Amendment to the US Constitution, the Prohibition Amendment. While both Catholics and Protestants considered drunkenness to be sinful, only Protestants, and conservative Protestants at that, considered all recreational drinking of alcoholic beverages to be of a sinful character. (An occasional sip of brandy for medicinal purposes was something else.) By the early twentieth century the USA, thanks to abundant immigration, had tens of millions of citizens—especially Italians, Irish Catholics, Germans of any religion, and Jews—who considered the drinking of beer, wine, etc. to be a normal part of adult life. Conservative Protestants had a very different view. They focused on the enormous harm done by drunkenness, especially the drunkenness of men who were husbands and fathers: the waste of scant family income in saloons, the wife-beating that drunk husbands often engaged in, and the neglect of children. If we can put a stop drinking, think how many social evils will be averted. Besides, conservative Protestants, for the most part rural or small-town Baptists and Methodists of Anglo-Saxon stock, were not fond of the drinking classes, who were largely urbanites and were either immigrants or the children of immigrants. The Prohibition movement was as much an anti-foreigner movement as it was an anti-drink movement.

While the Prohibition era, which lasted from 1920 to 1933, was probably effective to some extent in lowering the national level of drinking, drunkenness, and domestic abuse arising from drink, it was far more effective in producing contempt for the law (since vast numbers of people disregarded the law and kept on drinking), organized criminal gangs (who supplied the illegal drink), murder (as criminal gangs went to war with one another), and political corruption (as mayors and cops and judges took bribes to look the other way). While not many people took notice of the beneficial effects of Prohibition, nobody could avoid noticing the many harmful effects. In the elections of November 1932 the nation elected a "wet" president (FDR) and Congress, and by the end of 1933 a Repeal Amendment had been added to the Constitution.

Conservative Protestantism (by now widely referred to as "fundamentalism") had suffered an enormous defeat. The whole Prohibition experience caused its reputation to suffer an enormous blow, a second and perhaps even worse blow on top of the enormous blow it had suffered as a result of the "monkey trial" of 1925. This latter had been the unfortunate result of an earlier attempt to Christianize the nation, or at least to prevent its de-Christianization, by means of governmental action—the passing of state laws prohibiting the teaching of evolution in schools.

For the next few decades fundamentalists (or "Evangelicals," as they were increasingly coming to call themselves) decided that they would not try to use politics to Christianize and morally improve the nation. For one thing, they could probably not have much success, so low had their national reputation sunk by now as a result of Prohibition and anti-evolution laws. But for another, they had become convinced that this was not the best way to do things. Converting the nation, whether religiously or morally, was something better done on a one-by-one basis. Convert this person, and then the next person, and so on; and when enough persons have been converted over a long period of years and decades and maybe even centuries, the USA will be a strongly Christian and morally good nation. And so conservative Protestants withdrew from politics—not in the sense that they withdrew as individuals from voting and running for office; no, they kept doing that, just as other Americans did. But they no longer hoped to use their collective strength to create laws and government policies favorable to the advance of Christianity.

დ◦ ◦დ

Then came Roe v. Wade, the sensational US Supreme Court abortion ruling of 1973 according to which the US Constitution contains an implied right to abortion. In a single hour every anti-abortion law in the country, that is, every law intended to protect the lives of unborn babies, was struck down, declared to be unconstitutional.

At first Evangelicals didn't know how to respond to this earth-shaking ruling; the principal immediate objectors to the decision were, not themselves, but the Catholic episcopacy. Before much time went by, however, evangelical opposition to abortion grew and soon became stronger than Catholic opposition.

How could Evangelicals not be opposed? Thoughts like the following came to fill many an evangelical mind.

1. The Roe decision was in an important sense the climax of the sexual revolution, for it gave Constitutional protection to the most extreme consequence of the revolution's principle of sexual freedom. In effect, it said that American women are free to commit homicide in their pursuit of sexual freedom: not just any kind of homicide, to be sure, only the killing of unborn children.

2. What's more, since Americans have always been in the habit of thinking of human rights as God-given rights, the Roe ruling, by declaring that the right to abortion is a fundamental human right, was, practically speaking, telling Americans that women have a God-given right to kill their unborn babies.

3. But if we approve of the gigantic sin of abortion we will also have to approve—if we are to be logically consistent—of all kinds of lesser sins connected with sexuality. We'll have to approve of fornication and adultery and homosexuality and incest. It makes little sense to say, "I'm opposed to these latter sins, but I have no objection to abortion." That's like saying, "I'm opposed to shoplifting from candy stores, but I have no objection to bank robbery."

4. Giving legal sanction to the crime of abortion, which is what Roe v. Wade does, will not only result in an immense amount of sexual sin, but it will produce a general decline in American moral standards.

5. Traditional Protestantism, the Protestantism of Luther and Calvin and the other Reformers, was a religion that had always stressed chastity. It didn't stress it quite as much as Catholicism had, since Protestantism disapproved of monasticism, and didn't demand clerical celibacy, and didn't absolutely prohibit divorce. All the same, it had always placed a very heavy emphasis on chastity, making it one of the principal Christian virtues.

6. To give moral approval of abortion is in effect to give moral approval of unchastity generally. But to approve of unchastity generally is to repudiate traditional Protestantism; it is to repudiate much of the moral content of the old Protestant Consensus. And to repudiate a substantial portion of the Protestant Consensus is to become a liberal Protestant, if not a downright non-Christian.

Thoughts like these, I suggest, soon passed through the minds of many an Evangelical, and especially the minds of evangelical leaders, upon learning that the US Supreme Court, misreading the US Constitution in furtherance of the sexual revolution that had been sweeping the country for the previous decade or so, had decided that women have a right to kill their unborn babies. It was soon clear that Evangelicals would have to take a stand against abortion. For if they didn't, they would be failing to take a defensive stand against a great attack on Christianity.

But what caused the initial moments of hesitation? Why did they allow Catholics, not themselves, to offer the earliest resistance?

Evangelicals had a sense, I suggest, that to oppose abortion would require a return to politics; it would require them to abandon the attitude they had adopted ever since the twin disasters of Prohibition and laws against the teaching of biological evolution—the attitude that said, "We will lead people to Christ one by one, without the assistance of pro-Christian legislation or government action." Roe, that intolerable ruling, had been handed down by a government agency, the US Supreme Court. In theory, the Court is a non-political institution, and members of the Court are non-political. The justices may have had political biases, even strong political biases, earlier in their lives, but they are supposed to have left these at the door upon entering the Court. That's the theory, but as a matter of fact, probably quite unintentionally and perhaps quite unconsciously, they retain some of these earlier political biases. Even while wearing black robes they remain political animals. More, they are placed on the Court by politicians, that is to say, by men and women who stand for election—first of all, by the President of the USA, who nominates them, and secondly by the US Senate, which confirms them. And so, if the Roe decision is ever to be reversed, it will have to be done through politics. "We the opponents of abortion," Evangelicals said to themselves, "will have to get an anti-Roe majority on the Court; and to do that we'll have to get anti-Roe candidates elected to the presidency and to the US Senate. This will be a long-term project; it will take us many years, probably many decades, perhaps many generations, and perhaps a few centuries."

◠◠◠

By the late 1970s the Rev. Jerry Falwell had created "the Moral Majority," and in the 1980 presidential election he had thrown this organization's considerable support behind Ronald Reagan's candidacy. From that point on, Evangelicals, precisely *qua* Evangelicals, have been a major force in American politics—a major force allied with the Republican Party In the 2016 presidential election, more than 80 percent of self-identified Evangelicals voted for Donald Trump, who rewarded them during his term in office by nominating many "originalist" (and therefore presumably anti-Roe) judges to federal court seats, including the nomination of three originalist justices to the Supreme Court—Neil Gorsuch, Brett Kavanaugh, and Amy Coney Barrett. These many anti-Roe judges and justices were then duly confirmed by the Republican-dominated US Senate—sometimes in the face of furious opposition from pro-abortion forces.

In the 2020 presidential election evangelical voters continued to give Trump their overwhelming support. Many voters who had voted for Trump in 2016 drifted away from him in 2020. But not Evangelicals. They stuck with him. And their support mostly had to do with the fact that he promised to appoint anti-abortion (or pro-life) judges to the federal courts, above all the US Supreme Court. As I write these sentences (in 2022), there is every reason to believe that in 2024 evangelical voters will vote for Trump (if he runs again) or a Trump-like candidate.

Critics of Trump and critics of Evangelicals[2] often accuse evangelical supporters of Trump of being guilty of hypocrisy. They profess to be Christians, the critics point out, yet they are enthusiastic supporters of a man who has been divorced twice and married three times; who has admitted and even boasted about his adulteries; who by his bankruptcies has "stiffed" many creditors; who is vain, who is prideful, who is boastful, who is easily angered, who is prone to vengeance; who appears to have no more than a minimal acquaintance with the Bible—in short, a man who is anything but a model Christian; a far cry from a genuine evangelical Christian like President Jimmy Carter. In reply to such criticism we can easily imagine an Evangelical saying:

> I grant that Mr. Trump is not exactly a model Christian. I
> even grant that he's a long, long way from being a model

---

2. These two categories of critics overlap to a great degree. If you dislike Trump you probably disapprove of Evangelicals, and vice versa.

Christian. And I won't bother arguing with you if you want to say he's the very opposite of a model Christian. But it's not the least bit hypocritical of me to support him, and to support him from Christian motives. If these were good times I would not support him. I would find his moral shortcomings more than I could bear. But these are not good times. In the USA today Christianity is under assault from atheists, agnostics, and persons who are Christian in name only. It is under assault from great multitudes who are pro-fornication, pro-adultery, pro-abortion, pro-homosexuality, pro-same-sex marriage, pro-transgender, not to mention people who are pro-euthanasia and pro-recreational drug use. These anti-Christian forces are at work today restricting our freedom of religion and freedom of speech, and it is plain that they hope to go much further in the future. They are out to seduce our children and grandchildren into immoral and even unnatural sexual practices, and to draw them away from our Lord and Savior Jesus Christ. If Christianity is not to disappear in America, we have no choice but to fight back. And to fight, we need a leader. Trump, I admit, is far from an ideal leader. But he supports many (though not all) of our values, even if it may be that he doesn't share them in his heart of hearts. Moreover, he has that indispensable quality needed in a leader in a time of trouble—*a willingness to fight*. Of him we can say what Lincoln said of General Grant when critics complained of Grant's drinking habits. "I need him," Lincoln said, "he fights." So far from being a hypocrite by supporting Trump, I am just the opposite. Only the sincerity of my Christian faith could drive me to support so unappealing a champion as Donald Trump. I'd be a hypocrite if, having proclaimed my devotion to Jesus Christ, I allowed the religion of Jesus to die in America because the only champion I could find didn't have a clean enough heart and mind.

Let me summarize. Following a pattern that has been in place in the USA for more than two centuries now, evangelical Protantism—in other words, the traditional Protestantism that has preserved the five-hundred-hundred-year-old Protestant

Doctrinal Consensus—has responded in its usual way to the latest great crisis to hit American Protestantism, the sexual revolution. And what is involved in that "usual way"? It involves a rejection of the revolution both in its secular humanist (or atheistic) form and in its "Christianized" form. And it is a rejection without compromise. Evangelicals have been unwilling to say anything like: "Oh, let's have a little bit of fornication, and let's have a little bit of abortion, and let's have a little bit of homosexuality." They have sensed that once you open the door a "little bit" people will push the door open all the way, and before long Christian sexual morality will be destroyed completely. And they have sensed too that once Christian sexual morality is destroyed, what will follow sooner or later is the destruction of the entire Protestant Consensus. The have sensed, in other words, that the battle regarding sexual freedom is a battle for the survival of Christianity in America.

In saying that Evangelicals have rejected the sexual revolution "without compromise," I don't mean that this absence of compromise can be found in each and every Protestant who identifies as an Evangelical. Of course not. At the level of practice, many have compromised; that is to say, many evangelical individuals, including more than a few evangelical pastors, inspired by the atmosphere of sexual permissiveness that has permeated the USA for decades now, have committed sexual sins—they have engaged in fornication, adultery, homosexual sodomy; they have spent many hours watching pornography on their computers or smartphones; they have had abortions. But this kind of misconduct has been taking place for countless centuries; it didn't commence only with the coming of the sexual revolution. Who can doubt, however, that the revolution contributed to a notable increase, probably a tremendous increase, in these kinds of bad behavior?

More rare but not unknown have been compromises at the level of theory. Here and there and now and then, there have been evangelical pastors, theologians, and seminary students who have expressed sympathy with the idea that Christianity must learn to tolerate homosexual practice on the part of persons who were "born that way." But these people are exceptions, relatively rare exceptions, not the rule among Evangelicals. And if we are to judge from what has happened again and again in the long history of conservative Protestantism, these dissenters will eventually either return to the orthodox fold or depart from the evangelical world and become outright liberal Protestants.

What's more, if they wish to fight in defense of Christianity in America, Evangelicals have little choice but to conduct that fight on battlefields chosen by the enemies of Christianity—which is to say, secular humanists (atheists and agnostics) and their liberal Christian fellow travelers. In the decades since World War II, and especially since the 1960s, secular humanists and their fellow-travelers have steadily but surely seized control of America's great organs of moral and political propaganda—the journalistic mass media (both print and electronic), the entertainment industry (popular music, movies, TV), higher education, and even public schools. In addition to all of these, secular humanists and their allies have taken control of one of America's two great political parties, the Democratic Party—a control that is now so complete that the Democratic Party today may be described, with hardly any exaggeration, as an anti-Christianity party.[3]

And so we find Evangelicals struggling to construct organs of propaganda that communicate a message than contradicts the messages communicated by the organs of propaganda controlled by secular humanists and their allies—or, if they cannot construct these alternative organs, they at least patronize them when they happen to find them. Thus we find that Evangelicals provide much of the viewership for such cable news networks as Fox News, One America News (OAN), and Newsmax. And we find that evangelical parents of young children are more and more keeping their kids away from public schools, homeschooling them instead or sending them to private schools; and the parents of older children are sending their sons and daughters to colleges that profess to be Christian, not a few of these colleges being newly founded. There is a flourishing industry of Christian pop music, as well as a flourishing Christian publishing industry. Perhaps most noteworthy of

3. See my book, *Can a Catholic Be a Democrat?*

all, Evangelicals are almost universally committed to the political party that is the foe of the Democratic Party, which Evangelicals feel to be an anti-Christianity party, if not a downright Satanic party; in other words, they are almost unanimous in their support for the Republican Party.

Another way of putting this would be to say that Evangelicals are attempting to construct a "counter-world" to the anti-Christian "world" that has been constructed by secular humanists and their liberal Christian allies in the USA during the past half-century or so. If Evangelicals wish to encourage themselves in this effort at world-building, they can remind themselves, with some justice, that this effort of theirs is not unlike the effort made by early Christians to construct a counter-world to the pagan and morally corrupt world of the Roman Empire. That earlier effort, like to-day's effort, was an arduous uphill struggle, but in the end—after a few centuries of trying—it was successful. Well, more or less successful, for of course many of the pagans who finally entered the church did so while carrying remnants of paganism and moral corruption with them.

15

Where Do We Go from Here?

WHAT IS THE FUTURE of liberal Protestantism in the United States? Unfortunately for me or anybody else who would like to be a prognosticator, the future of society is always unpredictable. I have no magic crystal ball. All I can do is make a few guesses—well-informed guesses, I hope, but guesses all the same.

The liberal Protestant, I contend, is on slippery slope that leads downhill to atheism, either quite explicit atheism or the implicit atheism of the person who says he/she is an agnostic. Some liberals slide all the way down this slope during their lifetimes. Others don't go all the way, but their children or grandchildren do. For if you don't really believe in Christianity, it is difficult to pass on your "faith" to your children.

With regard to American religion, there are two logically consistent positions. (a) Secular humanism (or atheism), which totally rejects Christianity. Or (b) old-fashioned Christianity, which can be found in three forms: evangelical Protestantism, traditional Catholicism, and Eastern Orthodoxy (Greek, Russian, etc.). Liberal Protestantism (and liberal Catholicism for that matter) is a third thing. But this third things is logically inconsistent; it is unstable; it cannot endure.

Will liberal Protestantism totally disappear in America—the way, for example, the Shakers have totally (or almost totally) disappeared? I don't think so. For there will always be some people in the USA who will feel the need for the kind of religion offered by liberal Protestantism. In particular I'm thinking of four categories of people.

- Protestants who yesterday were only a "little bit" liberal (rather like the young woman who was only a "little bit pregnant"), but today are much more liberal, and yet are not ready to leap into atheism. For all practical purposes they have ceased to believe in Christianity, but are not ready to admit this to themselves.

- Ex-Evangelicals who, attracted by (or should I say seduced by?) the charms of secular humanism, have grown disillusioned with evangelical Protestantism, but are not yet ready to jump to atheism. They need a halfway house, and this is what liberal Protestantism provides.

- Ex-Catholics who have become disillusioned with the Catholic church because of its unwillingness to "modernize." Many such persons move directly into a non-religious status. They are unable to become Protestants of any kind, since the only element of their Catholicism that they retain is an old prejudice against Protestantism. Others, however, not willing to abandon Christianity altogether, realize they must turn to Protestantism. But evangelical Protestantism is quite unthinkable to them. So they turn to a liberal denomination. Often this is a liberal Episcopal church, for it reminds them of what they feel are the least objectionable aspects of their old religion. I can imagine a day when the liberal wing of the Episcopal church will be made up almost totally of ex-Catholics.

- Ex-secular humanists who have discovered in themselves a hunger for religion, but who feel that the move to evangelical Protestantism or to orthodox Catholicism would be too radical a departure from their previous atheism. Many of these, after having tried liberal Protestantism for a while, will realize that liberal religion is too similar to the atheism they fled, and so they will eventually move either to an evangelical church or to an orthodox Catholic church.

In any case, even though liberal Protestantism will survive, it will never again be what it once was in its glory days between the 1920s and the 1960s. That is to say, it will never again be America's unofficial national religion, its taken-for-granted religion. America's future will be either (a) traditional Christianity (evangelical Protestantism and orthodox Catholicism), with pockets of atheism here and there; or (b) atheism, with pockets of Christianity here and there.

It is unlikely that old-fashioned Christianity will be able to prevail over atheism unless Evangelicals and Catholics put aside their old animosities and learn to cooperate with one another. But will such "cooperation" be anything more than a further dose of the "ecumenism" that did so much damage to the mainline Protestant denominations in the course of the twentieth century by watering down Protestant doctrinal content in order to smooth the way to cooperation among the denominations? Perhaps—and if so, the Catholic-Evangelical alliance will be no more able to resist the advance of secularism than was the old intra-Protestant ecumenical alliance. But because Catholics and Evangelicals both have strong commitments to doctrinal purity and stability, and because they have maintained these commitments for many centuries, it is not beyond possibility that they may construct a practical alliance without watering down their doctrinal commitments.

After all, during World War II the western democracies, the USA and Britain, had a strong alliance with the Soviet Union despite the vast doctrinal gap that separated the democracies from Soviet communism—a gap much bigger than that between Catholic and evangelical doctrine. So great was the danger presented to both Russia and the democracies by the Axis powers that the two of them were willing, at least for the duration of the war, to keep relatively quiet about their ideological differences—but without giving up these differences. And of course as soon as the war was over the alliance dissolved, and the democracies and the communists went back to denouncing one another's doctrine.

When the Catholic-Evangelical alliance has soundly and definitively defeated secular humanism (something, I fear, that will not happen— if it ever does—for many centuries), the two parties can go back to denouncing one another. In the meantime much will be gained if Evangelicals say to themselves, "Those Catholics aren't so bad, and neither is their religion," while Catholics say to themselves, "Those Evangelicals aren't so bad, and neither is their religion." At the same time Evangelicals can remind one another of the doctrinal deficiencies of Catholicism while Catholics are reminding one another of the doctrinal deficiencies of evangelical Protestantism.

As a Catholic myself, I regret the breakup of Christian unity that took place at the time of the Reformation. But that was five hundred years ago. Today it is water over the dam. Today, I think, both sides, Catholic and evangelical, need one another. They need one another of course for what they have in common, for it is those common elements that will allow them to put up a more or less unified force in opposition to crusading atheism. Equally important, however, they need one another for those things on which they differ. Evangelicals can remind Catholics of what is lacking or insufficiently present in their own religion, and Catholics can remind Evangelicals of what is lacking or insufficiently present in their own religion. And each needs the criticisms of the other. The evangelical critique of Catholicism prevents Catholics from becoming too formal and legalistic in their Christianity, and the Catholic critique of evangelical Protestantism prevents Evangelicals from becoming too emotive and individualistic in their Christianity.

The danger of Catholic-Evangelical cooperation is, of course, that in order to assure better cooperation they will water down their differences; in other words, they will get rid of, in practice if not in theory, their doctrinal distinctiveness. This has happened in the past in intra-Protestant attempts at ecumenism: it has led in the direction of a kind of generic Protestantism in which doctrinal differences among denominations have been erased or at least semi-erased. However, there is good reason to believe that a practical alliance between Catholics and Evangelicals in the defensive fight against secular humanism (atheism) will not lead to a watering-down of their distinctive creeds. For if there are any religions that have a long historical record of very strong commitment to a set of doctrines, these religions are Roman Catholicism and evangelical Protestantism. Neither religion regards doctrine as one of its merely incidental features. Each regards doctrine—what it considers to be *divinely revealed true doctrine*—as one of its essential features. Neither is likely to regard doctrinal truth as something that can be hidden away in a closet in order to facilitate the fight against secular humanism.

Bibliography

Abbott, Lyman. *Henry Ward Beecher*. New York: Chelsea House, 1980.

———. *The Theology of an Evolutionist*. 1897. Reprint, London: Forgotten Books, 2016.

Allen, Ethan. *Reason, the Only Oracle of Man*. 1794. Reprint, Whitefish, MT: Kessinger, 2005.

Arnold, Matthew. *Literature and Dogma*. 1873. Reprint, New York: AMS, 1970.

———. "The Study of Poetry." In *Matthew Arnold: Selected Prose*, edited by P. J. Keating, 340–66. New York: Penguin, 1970.

Arnold, Thomas. *Principles of Church Reform*. 1833. Reprint, London: SPCK, 1962.

Bryan, William Jennings. *In His Image*. The James Sprunt Lectures. New York: Revell, 1922.

Buell, Lawrence, ed. *The American Transcendentalists: Essential Writings*. New York: Modern Library, 2006.

Carlin, David. *Can a Catholic Be a Democrat?* Manchester, NH: Sophia Institute, 2006.

———. *The Decline and Fall of the Catholic Church in America*. Manchester, NH: Sophia Institute, 2003.

Cartwright, Peter. *Autobiography*. Nashville: Abingdon, 1956.

Channing, William Ellery. *Selected Writings*. Edited by David Robinson. Mahwah, NJ: Paulist Press, 1985.

———. "Unitarian Christianity." In *Selected Writings*, 70–102. Mahwah, NJ: Paulist Press, 1985.

Darwin, Charles. *The Origin of Species*. 1859. Reprint, New York: Barnes & Noble, 2004.

Bibliography

Descartes, Rene. *A Discourse on Method and The Meditations*. Translated by F. E. Sutcliffe. London: Penguin, 1968.

Diderot, Denis, and Jean le Rond d'Alembert. *Encyclopedie*. Paris, 1751–66.

Emerson, Ralph Waldo. "The Divinity School Address." In *Ralph Waldo Emerson: Selected Essays*, edited by Larzar Ziff, 107. New York: Penguin, 1982.

———. "The Oversoul." In *Ralph Waldo Emerson: Selected Essays*, edited by Larzar Ziff, 205–24. New York: Penguin, 1982.

———. "The Problem." In *The American Transcendentalists: Essential Writings*, edited by Lawrence Buell, 451–53. New York: Modern Library, 2006.

———. "Self-Reliance." In *The Portable Emerson*, edited by Carl Bode and Malcolm Cowley, 138–64. New York: Penguin, 1981.

Finney, Charles Grandison. *Finney's Systematic Theology: The Complete and Newly Expanded 1878 Edition*. Minneapolis: Bethany, 1994.

Fiske, John. *The Idea of God as Affected by Modern Knowledge*. Boston: Houghton Mifflin, 1886.

Fletcher, Joseph. *Situation Ethics: The New Morality*. Louisville: Westminster, 1966.

Fosdick, Harry Emerson. "Shall the Fundamentalists Win?" http://baptiststudiesonline.com/wp-content/uploads/2007/01/shall-the-fundamentalists-win.pdf.

Freud, Sigmund. *Civilization and Its Discontents*. Translated by James Strachey. 1930. Reprint, New York: Norton, 1961.

Hodge, Charles. *What Is Darwinism?* 1874. Reprint, Grand Rapids: Baker, 1994.

James, William. *The Varieties of Religious Experience*. 1902. Reprint, New York: Penguin, 1982.

Jefferson, Thomas. *The Jefferson Bible: The Life and Morals of Jesus of Nazareth*. Boston: Beacon, 1984.

Kant, Immanuel. *Religion within the Limits of Reason Alone*. 1794. Translated by Theodore Greene and Hoyt Hudson. Reprint, New York: Harper Torchbooks, 1960.

Kramer, Stanley, dir. *Inherit the Wind*. Hollywood, CA: United Artists, 1960.

Larson, Edward. *A Summer for the Gods*. New York: Basic, 1997.

Leo XIII, Pope. *Rerum Novarum*. In *The Great Encyclical Letters of Pope Leo XIII*, 208–48. Rockford, IL: Tan, 1995.

Lessing, Gotthold. *Nathan the Wise*. Translated by Edward Kemp. London: Hern, 2015.

Locke, John. *Essay Concerning Human Understanding*. 1689. Reprint, Oxford: Oxford University Press, 1975.

———. *The Reasonableness of Christianity*. 1695. Reprint, Washington: Regnery Gateway, 1965.

Mansel, Henry Longueville. *The Limits of Religious Thought*. 1859. Reprint, London: Forgotten Books, 2018.

Mead, Margaret. *Coming of Age in Samoa*. New York: Morrow, 1928.

Miller, Perry, ed. *The American Transcendentalists*. Garden City, NY: Doubleday Anchor, 1957.

Bibliography

————, ed. *The Transcendentalists*. Cambridge, MA: Harvard University Press, 1950.

Miller, Perry, and Alan Heimert, eds. *The Great Awakening*. Indianapolis: Bobbs-Merrill, 1967.

Montaigne, Michel de. *Selected Esssays*. Translated by Charles Cotton, revised by W. Hazlitt and Blanchard Bates. New York: Modern Library, 1949.

Norton, Andrews. "A Discourse on the Latest Form of Infidelity." In *The Transcendentalists*, edited by Perry Miller, 210–13. Cambridge, MA: Harvard University Press, 1950.

Paine, Tom. *The Age of Reason*. 1794. Reprint, Secaucus, NJ: Citadel, 1974.

Paley, William. *Natural Theology*. 1802. Reprint, New York: Oxford's World Classics, 2008.

Parker, Theodore. *A Discourse on Matters Pertaining to Religion*. 5th ed. 1870. Reprint, London: Forgotten Books, 2012.

————. "A Discourse of the Transient and Permanent in Christianity." In *The Transcendentalists*, edited by Perry Miller, 259–83. Cambridge, MA: Harvard University Press, 1950.

Pascal, Blaise. *Pensées and Other Writings*. Translated by A. J. Krailsheimer. London: Penguin Classics, 1995.

Rauschenbusch, Walter. *Christianity and the Social Crisis*. New York: Macmillan, 1907.

Renan, Ernest. *The Life of Jesus*. New York: Modern Library, 1955.

Russell, Bertrand. *Marriage and Morals*. 1929. Reprint, New York: Bantam, 1959.

Smyth, Newman. *The Religious Feeling, a Study of Faith*. London: Ward, Locke, & Co., 1877.

Spencer, Herbert. *First Principles*. 2nd ed. 1867. Reprint, New York: DeWitt Revolving Fund, 1958.

Spong, John Shelby. *Living in Sin: A Bishop Rethinks Human Sexuality*. San Francisco: HarperSanFrancisco, 1988.

Torrey, R. A., et al. *The Fundamentals*. 1910–15. Reprint, Grand Rapids: Baker, 1998.

Voltaire. *Philosophical Dictionary*. 1764. Reprint, Mineola, NY: Dover, 2010.

Wikipedia. "Benjamin Franklin." https://en.wikipedia.org/wiki/Benjamin_Franklin.

————. "Joseph Fletcher." https://en.wikipedia.org/wiki/Joseph_Fletcher.

————. "Old-Time Religion." https://en.wikipedia.org/wiki/Old-Time_Religion.

Index

Index

Index

Printed in the USA
CPSIA information can be obtained
at www.ICGtesting.com
LVHW022314081223
765728LV00005B/124

9 781666 795097